GUIDE TO LIVING FRUITFUL GODLY PRODUCTIVE CHRISTIAN LIFE

Mary Olufunmilayo Adekson

NEW HARBOR PRESS

RAPID CITY, SD

Adekson/New HarborPress
1601 Mt. Rushmore Rd, Ste 3288
Rapid City, SD 57701
www.newharborpress.com

Ordering Information:
Quantity sales. Special discounts are available on quantity purchases by corporations, associations, and others. For details, contact the "Special Sales Department" at the address above.

Guide to Living Fruitful Godly Productive Christian Life/ Mary Olufunmilayo Adekson. -- 1st ed.

ISBN 978-1-63357-395-6

Guide me, O Thou great Jehovah,

Pilgrim through this barren land;

I am weak, but Thou art mighty;

Hold me with Thy powerful hand;

Bread of heaven, Bread of heaven,

Feed me till I want no more,

Feed me till I want no more.

John Hughes (1873-1932).

Lead kindly Light amid th'encircling gloom,

Lead Thou me on;

The night is dark, and I am far from home;

Lead Thou me on:

Keep Thou my feet;

I do not ask to see

The distant scene –one step enough for me.

John B. Dykes (1823-1876)

And I stand I stand in awe of you

I stand I stand in awe of you

Holy God to whom all praises due

I stand in awe of you !

{Mark Altrogge (1987)}

Dedication

GUIDE TO LIVING FRUITFUL *Godly Productive Christian life* is dedicated to Our Almighty Father who knows all things and assists all His children to successfully live for Him every day.

To all dedicated Christians all over the world. God loves you. He will give you wisdom to continue to be your best as His children with His guiding Hand.

To all those who will procure His guidance as they turn to Him today.

And to all my academic, physical and spiritual sons and daughters all over the world. Be blessed. You are highly favored by the Almighty God, your Papa.

Preface

GUIDE TO LIVING FRUITFUL *Godly Productive Christian Life* is written for all of us to show us that God is supreme. This guide will point us to things that we already know and also bring to mind things that we still need to ponder on as God's Children. The book will portray to all, young, middle-aged and old alike that God is available and ready to show His love to all of us and also guide us. You only need to acknowledge Him, and He will be close to your side. He will competently answer your prayers and take fatherly care of you throughout your abode here. His love endures forever! *Guide to Living Fruitful Godly Productive Christian life* discusses how mighty our God is and also points us to the names of God and shows us that our God is the God of more than enough. The guide encourages us to perceive the hindrances that can prevent us from being fruitful productive Christians and encourages us to value God's Word, prayer and the Holy Spirit and to also know that most detours lead us to the Promised Land. So, enjoy this guide and cherish it with examples from our fore-parents who have walked here before us. And if, as Hebrews 11 proclaims, they made it with all their flaws and shortcomings, we will all also make it in Jesus' Name.

Introduction

I ALWAYS COME IN contact with different people who ask me questions about this Almighty God that I love so much. This is especially true because of the fact that they notice that I am a Christian and that I show my love of the Father through my actions and words over the course of our conversations or interactions. As I say, God is excellent all the time! He is a true and faithful Father whose love is incomparable to none other. I was therefore moved to write *Guide to Living Fruitful Godly Productive Christian Life* from my experience to bring out some points about the love that Our Heavenly Father bestow on us and have for us as our Father, to discuss cogent points about the heart of man (and woman), discuss the ardent love of God, to sound a note of warning about looking for love in the wrong places and also point us to other important facets for living a fruitful productive life as God's child.

When we think of God so many things come to mind. Some of us think of God as one who disciplines us and one who is angry when we do not perform to His expectations like some of our earthly fathers expect. Some people even think that God is always looking for them to be perfectionists. That is, someone who can do all things perfectly before He can love them. These are all far from the truth. As we can see from the Word of God, God is loving, full of compassion and always ready to forgive and give us new beginnings. God is not only competent and reliable, He is also full of mercy and grace towards all of us. This is depicted in the fact that He pours down

His abundant rain and lets His sun and rain to shine and fall on the just and unjust and on the righteous and the unrighteous (Matthew 5:45; Luke 6:35-36). Yes, on all and sundry. Yes, on those who do His will and those who do not do His will. God is love! Some of the discussions in this guide will allow you to see the mighty hand of God as your father. And it will help those whose earthly father have disappointed them to perceive that God the Father loves them and He wants to have a relationship with them. There are also discussions on important characteristics of God as our Father. God is not only holy, knowledgeable and powerful, He is also fully committed to us and to our day-to-day welfare.

Our physical heart takes care of all the blood that flows throughout our body. It stands for the core of a person's being (Psalm 16:7). Have you ever thought about your spiritual heart? The heart is the very center of our being and the source from which everything proceeds. Our spiritual heart has the capacity to make or unmake us as Christ's followers and as human beings. Some ardent points are raised in this guide about what flows spiritually through your heart. As I was ruminating on what permeates in our hearts as human beings, I was just thinking about both the kindness, love and compassion as well as the atrocities and wickedness that exudes from the heart of human beings one person to another. These all stem from the heart. For out of the heart springs love, peace, longsuffering, compassion, kindness, goodness, faithfulness, gentleness and self-control; but also, deceit, adultery, fornication, uncleanness, lewdness, sorcery, hatred, contentions, jealousies, outbursts of wrath, selfish ambitions, dissensions, heresies, envy, murders, drunkenness, revelries, wickedness, idolatry, and the like, etc. (Galatians

5:22-23; 19-20; Jeremiah 17:9; Mark 7:21-23). These aforementioned emotions are also classified as fruits of the Spirit and works of the flesh in the Word of God. As a born- again Christian, I find my answers to what plagues the heart of man and stirs up the heart of man and encourages man to bear good fruits in the Holy Bible and the leadings of the Holy Spirit. The answers to curing man's atrocities and also to being filled with love, are not in any other thing but in accepting the Lord Jesus as your Lord and Savior and in reading and understanding the Word of God. The Word cleanses and washes the heart clean (2 Timothy 3:16-17). God is the main cure of infirmities of the heart where it occurs. This does not mean only physical infirmities but also spiritual infirmities. The heart is deceitful above all else, (Psalm 51:10 &12; 32; Jeremiah 17:9; John 21:15-19; Acts 22:6-16) and God cannot be mocked whatsoever a man (or a woman) sows he (or she) shall reap (Galatians 6:7; Psalm 62:12). If sin or failure has fragmented your heart and soul, confess it to God and let Him restore to you the joy of your salvation (Psalm 51:12). God is the ultimate restorer. He will restore the pieces of your life. God completely remakes a person on the inside and allow a woman or a man to put on the new nature (Ephesians 4:24) after you accept Jesus Christ as your Savior.

God remakes you and puts His confidence into your life and recreates you to have a heart of gratitude, love, compassion and kindness (Galatians 5:22-23). "God does not take our natural virtues and transform them, because our natural virtues could never even come close to what Jesus Christ wants" us to be (Oswald Chambers). As Oswald Chambers continued: "no natural love, no natural patience, no natural purity can ever come up to His demands, and every virtue we possess is His alone." God's mercy and grace cleanses our sins and blots out our past mistakes. It is in God's forgiveness that we see our heart glow with repentance and love from our Savior and Father. Your heart and mind gains freedom from God's forgiveness from Calvary's love. And when love come out of your heart you realize as Michael W. Smith reiterated that, "love wasn't put in your heart to stay. Love isn't love until you give it away." And through love you will serve one another (Galatians 5:13; John 13:3-5 & 15-17; John 13:1; 1 Corinthians 13). So, keep your heart with all diligence, for out of it springs the issue of life (Proverbs 4:23b). Oswald Chambers reiterated that, "if a sinner really wishes to understand his(or her) heart, let him (or her) listen to (her or) his mouth in an unguarded frame for five minutes." What are you constantly obsessed with every day of your life? This is what will be your main motive and your actions will be based on this small but significant fact. God sees our hearts and He can mend it if we come short and give Him room into our hearts. So, let God into your heart. Points are raised in the *Guide to living Fruitful Godly Productive Christian life* that will make you think about what you habor in your heart and allow you to make amends if needed. The section on having a heart that yearns for the Lord our Father, is therefore written to chastise you, to make you think about the love of God. They will give you the inspiration to know that God cares deeply about you His Creation and wants to give you a pure heart. Are you ready for this Spiritual Heart Surgery? Be blessed as you peruse the section that speaks about your heart as God's child and learn how you can have a pure and clean heart.

Another section of this guide also talks about God's love for us. It discusses the love that we enjoy from the Trinity: God the Father, God the Son and God the Holy Spirit. Oswald Chambers reiterated that "the love of God is not created---it is His nature." *Guide to living Fruitful Godly Productive Christian life* therefore admonishes us about looking for love in anything else but God. The points discussed in this section will assist you to see where you have waywardly deviate from God's love and compassion to go your own way. Some Christians have also strayed from the flock of Christ by looking for love in the wrong places. God who is love, shows us that we should look to Him for the love of our lives. Reading the Word, praying, listening to the Holy Spirit and being in fellowship with other believers, will permeately help us grow in the love of the Lord and dissuade us from looking in the wrong places for love that is of the world.

The section on so many detours and one destination; choices, life is full of choices; do your work as unto the Lord; bite your tongue, hold your peace, face adversity with courage and praying for the patience of Job, just echoes what we have all heard preached in different churches, by emphasizing the importance of making God a paramount source of our lives and living for Him in our daily interactions with others. So, peruse this valuable guide with your Bible by your side !

Who is Mary Olufunmilayo Adekson ?

MY CHILDHOOD WAS FULL of spiritual adventures after I accepted the Lord Jesus Christ as my Lord and Savior when I was 8 years old. My life has not been the same ever since I encountered my Lord. I remember clinging tightly to the beautiful picture of the lilies (Matthew 6:28-30) that my Sunday School Teacher gave us after her sermon to us about God's provision and care, that unforgettable and divine Sunday. I determined and resolved in my heart to love this Almighty Father who takes care of the lilies in the field which are here today and destroyed tomorrow. I possessed a childlike belief that this God is going to take care of me throughout my life here on earth. The rest is history. I was transformed with a dramatic vision of God with a personal relationship with Him and God has proved Himself to me over all these years and He still continues to deliver on His Promises. I go to Him for answers for all situations in my life. He listens and answers my cries, petitions and prayers. I am also grateful to my Godly earthly father, late Papa Gabriel Omodele Ekundiya Asanbe-Williams who stood by me during trials, troubles and tribulations. As Psalm 112 verse 6b says, "The righteous shall be in everlasting remembrance." Papa you are remembered for all your fatherly care for me and my family.

I am a walking miracle and remain a wonder unto many because of Jesus Christ who loves me. I am grateful to You God for the opportunity to know You and be a living witness for You. I stand!I stand in awe of You !! Holy God to whom all praise is due !!! I stand in awe of You !!!! Thank you so much God. You are AWESOME, HOLY, EXCELLENT and GREAT !!!!!

Contents

Embrace and acknowledge God as a Competent and Reliable Father

Who and what is a father?

A FATHER IS DEFINED as a man who has a child by a woman. An example of a father is one who has a son or a daughter or sons and daughters. A father is implored to bring their children up in the ways of the Lord, to discipline them, encourage, instruct and comfort them. Ephesians 6 verse 4 says that fathers should not provoke their children to anger but bring them up in the fear, discipline and admonition of the Lord. A good father loves his children and disciplines them with love that shows through his actions. Children should be able to enjoy peace, provision, comfort, rest, and consistent love from their fathers. A father is persistently there for his children and family in all circumstances. A father loves his children at all times. He teaches them to be a real child of God by living through godly example in front of them. A godly father models what our Father in Heaven is. Fatherhood entails love, identity, hope, and inspiration that fathers provide for their children. It is unfortunate that some earthly fathers show neglect in their duties to their offspring. At times earthly fathers disappoint or hurt their children. In some cases, some children of these fathers fail to see how God Our loving

Father could allow them to go through this kind of ordeal. In these cases, these feelings that give rise to emotional scars have left some growing up with a suspicious attitude towards God Almighty and everything that relates to Him. This unfortunate feeling, attitude and emotions take long years to subside even with constant assurance and love from God as their reliable and competent Creator and Father. Matthew 7 verse 11 that God reserves excellent things that even our earthly father cannot give us, for our daily enjoyment. Be assured that, as you will read in subsequent chapters, that God as Our Heavenly Father, is excellent, reliable, competent, abounding in love, compassionate, gracious, slow to anger, faithful (Psalm 103:8), and never fails in His doting on us as His children and creation.

Our Father is a God of love who can be trusted regardless of our current situation. "When we know that God's hand is in everything, we can leave everything in God's hand" (Philip Yancey, Our Daily Bread Ministries). Since we are wonderfully and fearfully created by God (Psalm 139:14), we are very very, special and we are His Masterpiece (Ephesians 2:10). And where our earthly fathers do not measure up, our Heavenly Father will fill the slack in our lives. All we have to do is let Him be our Father. Defer to Him and He will neither leave you nor forsake you (Deuteronomy 31:6 & 8). Look up, Look up, don't be frightened, Our Father understands, It will be well. Do not give up on your Heavenly Papa. Love him and He will envelope you with His love and attention and make up for all those neglect and unloving relationships.

God is our Heavenly Father? Our Omnipotent Father! Our Omnipresent Father!! Our Omniscience Father!!!

JESUS SAID THAT ANYONE who has seen Him has seen the Father (John 14:9). He went on to say that He is in the Father and the Father is in Him (John 14:10). If you want to know what God is like, look at Jesus Christ. God sees Himself in His Son (Matthew 3:17). Jesus pleases His Father. He is perfect and flawless. Jesus is love, He is compassionate, and He does not take sides. He is neither judgemental nor lacking in understanding. God is good!(Psalm 25:8). The cross is the barometer of God's goodness and love to us (John 3:16) not our circumstances or what we are currently going through. The more we trust God, the more we realize that God is excellent all the time. God who is majestic and much bigger than ourselves, crowned us with glory (Psalm 8:3-5; Revelation 21:22-25). The Lord exudes love, gentleness and patience towards us. As a father pities his children, so the Father pities them that fear Him (Psalm 103:13).

God is full of love, mercy, grace, abundance, forgiveness, contentment and joy (John 15:11). God is all sufficient in Himself that it spills into our lives as His children. God's promises are backed by His flawless character. David Egner of Our daily Bread Ministries reiterated that, "God's faithfulness dispels our fearfulness." In Psalm 36 verse 5, the Psalmist exclaims that, "thy mercy O Lord, is in the heavens, and thy faithfulness reaches unto the clouds." The Lord is our Shepherd (Psalm 23) who gives us all we need, renews our strength, guides us along the right paths, restores our souls and helps us to bring honor to His Name. Lisa Bevere reiterated that, "A good shepherd knows how to lead His sheep when they aren't sure where they are going" (Encouragement for Today). As Lisa continued, "no moment or place exists without His presence, (and) there has never been a space void of Him—not in your past, present or future." King David reveled in the wonder of God's intimate presence in Psalm 139 verses 5 to 7 when he blurted out: "You have hedged me behind and before and laid Your hand upon me. Such knowledge is too wonderful for me; It is high I cannot attain it. Where can I go from Your Spirit? Or where can I flee from your presence?" In letters to Malcolm, C. S. Lewis highlights this truth: "we may ignore but we nowhere evade, the presence of God. The world is crowded with Him. He walks everywhere incognito." All that is in the universe declares God's grandeur and majesty. Our Father reassures us and holds us up when we are down as we regain our balance. God helps and assists us to gain our joy, strength and confidence when we feel helpless and hopeless and without comfort. God is the God of all comfort who has compassion on those who fear Him (Psalm 103:13). Sper reiterated that "when you are tempted to deny God's goodness, love, and grace, look to the cross of Calvary, when Jesus took your place."

And you are blessed and highly favored by your Heavenly Father who is Omnipresent because He is ever present and He will never leave us nor forsake us (Psalm 139:7-12). He is Omnipotent because He is the all- powerful Creator who created us in His own image (Psalm 139:13-18). And He is Omniscient for His knowledge of everything about us is immesurable (Psalm 139:1-6). God is everywhere (Psalm 139:7-12). Whether we are sitting at home, or flying miles above the earth, He is ever present with us and over us all the time. This should make us trust in His loving assurance. God is always present to guide, provide for us and protect us. And you know what, God has promised to establish His covenant with you as He promised to do with Isaac (Genesis 17:21). And He who has begun a good work in you will complete His blessings in your life with the help of Our Lord Jesus Christ (Philippians 1:6). God is our Creator and the Creator of the Universe. We are His creation and He created us for a purpose. The All-Wise, benevolent and omnipotent God is a wise and excellent Creator. Prophet Isaiah reiterated that God brings out the stars and calls each of them all by name (Isaiah 40:25-26). Isaiah added that "by the greatness of His might and the strength of His power, not one is missing" (Isaiah 40:26). This our Father, who knows the stars by name and takes care of them, knows us individually and personally as His Masterpiece and He keeps us under His watchful care (Isaiah 40:27). Our Father loves us and takes excellent care of us with His wisdom and power. And He is able to make all grace abound towards us (2 Corinthians 9:8). His comforting presence is with us throughout our lives. God is awesome, high and exalted above all gods (Psalm 92:1-15; Exodus 15:1-21; Job 36:22; Isaiah 33:5-6; Psalm 93:1). John Piper says, "there is no power in the universe that can stop God from fulfilling His totally good plans for you." God is always doing more than we know on our behalf. He is always working toward your good and keeping you rooted in Him. Secure yourself in God not in fellow humans. God who is unchanging and undeniably great has excellent intentions for your life and your family members lives if they are His (Jeremiah 29:11-13). So, surrender your all--- talents, gifts, efforts, and service to Him. God will hear you and maintain your cause (1 Kings 8:49). Trust God and your cup will overflow with His blessings (Psalm 23:5; 103:2 & 3-4). Our God will do all He promises He will do in your life. He is our everlasting Father. The Lord knows all those that are His (2 Timothy 2:19).

Our Heavenly Father is far more intimately acquainted with each of His children. He is aware of every thought, emotion, and decision we make. He oversees us 24/7. The Psalmist says, "such knowledge is too wonderful for me, it is high, I cannot attain it" (Psalm 139:6). This should make us shout Halleluia! Jesus reiterated that not even a sparrow falls without the knowledge of our Papa (Matthew 10:29). He knows all the strands in our hair. And He pointed out that we are of more value than the birds or lilies (Matthew 6:25-34). We are more precious in our Father's eyes. In every endeavor, big or small, we can trust God's heart towards us. Jesus who has a perfect heart to bestow us with His blessings and excellent plans, and the One who has conquered death and given us new life (2 Corinthians 5:17), will make all things new in our lives (Psalm 23:4). We could never conceive or imagine the plans He has towards us (Genesis

32:24). He is our everlasting Father, who neither grows tired nor weary and whose understanding no-one can fathom (Isaiah 40:28).

Know God! Rely on Him totally not on any other person and your life will take a positive turn for the best. Let the Words of God make you a better child of the Almighty. As a limited being we should look to the abundance of our limitless Father who knows all things and who can do all things. In our finiteness we must learn to accept the mysteries of His power, mightiness and greatness and also covet His infinite love (Isaiah 55:8-13). Hide yourself in Him. Spend more time with God in prayer and meditation and a deeper digging into His Word. Acknowledge God's greatness as you pray and interact with Him. You are an anointed child of the Almighty.

Do not go to anyone to get that fact. Most people do not have the same relationship you have with your Father now. So, cherish this relationship and do not go to anyone for the blessings that God has solely reserved for you. You are His anointed and spokesperson and He wants to use you and carry out His plan through you. Do not throw away your confidence because in quietness and confidence is your strength (Isaiah 30:15c). The joy of the Lord is your strength (Nehemiah 8:10) and you are a conqueror now (Romans 8:37) and you will always be a conqueror. So, go on your knees when you have a need or a request. Jesus died for your sins and for your sake and you can approach your Papa with this confidence as your base. He blessed all our fore-parents in the faith and He is waiting for you to ask for your blessings. He will do for you what your friends and anybody else cannot do. So, approach the throne of mercy and be blessed today and every day.

The fact that you have accepted Jesus Christ as Your Lord and Savior gives you access to God as your Father since God loves His Son and sent Him to die for our sins. He counts us worthy and righteous because of this. God's love for us is pure, perfect, and rooted in the way He loves His Son. John 3 verse 16 says, "For God so loved the world that He gave His only begotten Son that whoever believes in Him should not perish but have everlasting life." And John 6 verse 33 says Jesus is the bread of life that came down from heaven to give life to the world. So, wherever you go in this world God's eyes go with you and follow you to protect and care for you because His promise is: He will neither leave you nor forsake you (Deuteronomy 31:6 & 8). So, know one thing, He has excellent plans for your life whatsoever you are engaged in right now in your abode here. All you have to do is seek Him and His righteousness and all other things will be added to you (Matthew 6:33). And Our Father will rejoice over you (Zephaniah 3:17) and keep you as the apple of His eye and hide you under the shadow of His wings (Psalms 17:8). So, what are you waiting for to be counted worthy of this never-ending love if you don't think you are counted worthy now? To be counted as apple of God's eye bow your head now or kneel where you are and ask Jesus to be your Lord and Savior. And you will be secure in God's Arms and become the apple of God's eye and all things will become new in your life (2 Corinthians 5:17). If you are already His Child and have accepted Jesus Christ as your Lord and Savior, continue in His Love by being pure and being led by the Holy Spirit.

What do you call Him?

God's Names reveal a precious truth about His qualities and character. You call Him Father. You call Him the Almighty. You call

Him Jehovah. He is the Most High. God is Our Father/Abba. God has been called different Names in the Holy Bible. I will briefly mention some of these Names here. He is Jehovah Jireh (The Lord will provide) (Genesis 22:14; Philippians 4:19). Jehovah Nissi (The Lord My Banner) (Exodus 17:13-16). Jehovah Shalom (The Lord is Peace) (Judges 6:24; Isaiah 26:3). He is Elohim (Sovereign and Omnipotent God) (Genesis 6:9; Hebrews 11:5-6; Psalm 139). He is El Shaddai (Lord God Almighty; the All-Powerful God) (Genesis 17:1; Psalm 91:1). He is El Elyson (The Most High God) (Psalm139). Adonai (Lord Master; Sovereign Father) (Psalm 86). Yahweh (Lord Jehovah) (Deuteronomy 33:26-29; Exodus 15:1-18). Jehovah Raah (The Lord My Shepherd) (Psalm 23). Jehovah Rapha (The Lord that Heals) (Exodus 15; Psalm 23; Psalm 103:3). Jehovah Shammah (The Lord is There)(Ezekiel 48:35; Revelation 21-22). Jehovah Mekoddishkem (The Lord Who Sanctifies You)(Leviticus 20:7-8). Jehovah Tsidkenu (The Lord Our Righteousness) (Jeremiah 23:6). El Olam (The Everlasting God) (Genesis 21:33). Quanna (Jealous, Zealous) (Exodus 20:5; 34:14; Deuteronomy 4:24; 5:9; 6:15). Jehovah Sabaoth (The Lord of Hosts; The Lord of Armies) (1 Samuel 1:3). El Roi (The God who sees me) (Genesis 16:13; Psalm 139:16). Jehovah Eli (My God) (Psalm 18:2). Jehovah Elohenu (Our God) (Exodus 8:10). Jehovah-Gibbor Michamah (Mighty in Battle) (Psalm 24:8). Jehovah Go'el (Redeemer) (Isaiah 49:26, 60:16). Jehovah Hamelech (The King) (Psalm 98:6). Jehovah Hashopet (The Judge) (Judges 11:27). Jehovah Hoshe'ah (The Lord Who Saves) (Psalm 20:9). Jehovah Izuz Gibbor (Strong and Mighty) (Psalm 24:8). Jehovah Kabodhi (My Glory) (Psalm 3:3). Jehovah Keren Yish'l (Horn of my Salvation) (Psalm 18:2). Jehovah Machai (My Refuge) (Psalm 91:9). Jehovah Magen (The Shield) Deuteronomy 33:29). Jehovah Makeh (The Lord who strikes you) (Ezekiel 7:9). Jehovah Ma'ozi (My Fortress) (Jeremiah 16:19). Jehovah Mekoddishkem (The Lord Who Makes you Holy; The Lord who sanctifies you) (Leviticus 20:7-8; Exodus 31:3). Jehovah Melech'Olam (King Forever) (Psalm 10:16). Jehovah Mephalti (My Deliverer) (Psalm 18:2) and Jehovah Moshl'ech (Your Savior) (Isaiah 49:26, 60:16). I AM WHO I AM (Exodus 3:14). YAH (Psalm 68:4). God our Ebenezer (Hitherto has He helped us) (1 Samuel 7:12). You call Him Abba Father and Papa, who calls you the apple of His eye (Deuteronomy 32:10; Zechariah 2:8). "For the Lord your God is a merciful God" (Deuteronomy 4:31). The Lord God Almighty (Revelation 4:8), is a term that means "powerful and immovable." Julie Schwab of Our Daily Bread Ministries reiterated that, "additionally, God's eternality and authority are reflected in the reference to Him as the One who was and is and is to come." God is worthy of the praise of His creation (Revelation 4:11). You can call Him any or all of these names when you pray. We are dependent upon His revelation of His nature to understand Him. We must have reverence for God's Name so that others who hear us admire and respect Him will esteem Him with us.

You know what! You are so special to your Almighty Father the Creator of all things. The "father to the fatherless and a defender of widows" (Psalm 68:5a). So, ask yourself: What makes me so special? Of course, the answer is obvious. The fact that you have accepted Jesus Christ as Your Lord and Savior gives you access to God as your Father since God loves His Son and sent Him to die for our sins. He counts us worthy and righteous because of this. God's love for us is pure, perfect, and rooted in the way He loves His Son. So, the Almighty, your Father whose names are multiple, more than all the names I wrote above, has excellent plans for your life whatsoever you are engaged in right now in your abode here. He has time for you too. Speak to Him who has a name that is universal with no limitations, about what ails you. He is more than enough for you.

Who can you compare Him to? Who can compare to Him?

God, who spoke the Universe into existence (Genesis 1), and who rules and stills the raging of the sea when its waves rise (Psalm 89:9), is unlike no one. "For since the beginning of the world men have not heard nor perceived by the ear nor has the eye seen any God beside You, Who acts for the one who waits for Him" (Isaiah 64:4). "O God You are more awesome than Your holy places. The God of Israel is He who gives strength and power to His people" (Psalm 68:35). God displays His marvelous love to us (1 John 3:1a). He showed us incomprehensible love through the sacrifice of His sinless Son, Jesus Christ for us sinners (John 3:16). This sacrifice allows us easy access to the throne of grace and to God Our Heavenly Father. God, a father to the fatherless (Psalm 68:5-6) and a husband to the widow is incomparable to no one. God is the one we can embrace without reservation or hinderance. "Your mercy O lord is in the heavens, Your faithfulness reaches to the clouds (and). Your righteousness is like the great mountains; Your judgements are a great deep, O Lord, You preserve man and beast" (Psalm 36:5-6).

Moses vibrant words in Exodus 15 verse 11: Who is like unto thee O Lord! Who is like unto thee? among the gods who is like thee, glorious in holiness and fearful in praises, doing wonders Halleluia, sums up the point that there is none like our Lord there is no one like Him. None, and I mean no one, can compare with Our loving Heavenly Father. He is the All in All. The I Am that I Am. As you can see from His Names in the previous chapter, He is all we need. There is no one that can stand in His front or at His back or below or above Him. Isaiah said in ruminating about what Our Father said, in Isaiah 40 verses 18 and 25 that, "To whom then will you liken Me, or to whom Shall I be equal? says the Holy One."

Know one thing, He who created the world has you covered (Revelation 4:11). And He is God!There is none like Him. Declaring the end from the beginning, and from ancient times things that are not yet done. Saying His counsel shall stand. And He will do all His pleasure (Isaiah 46:9-10). The hands that control the universe----God's hands-----are wise and compassionate. We can trust these hands in spite of our circumstances and not be afraid. That is Our Papa who reigns from everlasting to everlasting. Our Almighty Father is mightier than all. To God belongs wisdom and might (Daniel 2:20-21). "The Lord is King!He is robed in majesty. Indeed, the Lord is robed in majesty and armed with strength. The world stands firm and cannot be shaken" (Psalm 93:1). "Your throne is established from of old. You are from everlasting" (Psalm 93:2). "What a mighty God we serve. (Halleluia !). Angels bow before Him. Heaven and earth adore Him. What a mighty God we serve. He holds the winds in His Hand and He is the great I am. He is the bright and morning star. And without Him I would fall. Jahovah Jirah, my provider. Jahovah Shiloh, my peace. Jahovah Signanu, my righteousness" (Songwriter: Elder Eric Mcdaniels). Yes He is mighty and great!No one can stand in front, back, bottom or above our Great God !! "But the Lord is the great God. And the great King above all gods. In His hand are the deep places of the earth, the heights of the hills are His also. The sea is His, for He made it and His hands formed the dry land" (Psalm 95:3-5).

And this our God: for every beast of the forest is His. And the cattle on a thousand hills. He knows all the birds of the mountains and the wild beasts of the field are His (Psalm 50: 10-11). Our Father who created all that is in the Universe and owns all the riches of the vast Universe can be compared to no one. God is the self-existent One. He is the Creator and Sustainer. Nothing creates or sustains Him. He is the One true God distinct from all other gods. God who is majestic also affirms His personal concern for each of us His creation (Psalm 147:3,6,11; Psalm 8). "The God who made the firmament, who made the deepest sea, the God who put the stars in place. Is the God who cares for (us)" (Berg).

Biblical Scholar George Bush (1796-1859) wrote the following about God's description of Himself in Exodus 3 verse 14 as I AM WHO I AM: "He, in distinction from all others, is the one only true God, the God who really is...... The eternal, self-existent, and immutable Being; the only being who can say that He always will be what He always has been." Bow in reverence to the I AM WHO I AM, whose name is perfect for Him. Our All-Knowing, All Present, All Perfect Competent and Reliable Father who we adore.

Who can compete with Him?

There is none holy as the Lord for there is none beside thee. Neither is there any rock like our God (1 Samuel 2:2-3). There is none holy as the Lord. Michael W. Smith sang: "There is none like You!No one else can touch my heart like You do. I could search for all eternity long and find there is none like You." There is nobody that can compete with our God because there is none like Him. He has proved Himself to generations before us and He still continues to prove Himself as our strong dependent Father. We refer to Him as "Atofehinti" in Yoruba Nigerian language, which means a reliable One. That is, a Solid Rock that we can rely on. God is the Creator that we can depend on. In all the world history there has been no one, I mean no one that can stand in the place of God. There is going to be no one that can stand in His place. There is nobody as great as our God (Psalm 77:13). There is therefore no one who can compete with Him. No one has His power because He weaves all creation together. Our God declares that, He is God and there is no other and that there is none like Him (Isaiah 46:9).

He repays all for their deeds (Psalm 62:12) and He is waiting to judge us after our time here is spent. "Among the gods there is none like You, O Lord. Nor are there any works like Your works .....For You are great, and do wondrous things. You alone are God" (Psalm 86:8-10). So, we should do good and accept Jesus as our Lord and Savior, so we do not face His wrath. As our All-Sufficient Father who sustains us, He is the Master Planner and Master Designer whose spiritual vitality has no comparison. All our springs are in Him as our only source of life which no one can compare to (Psalm 87:7). God's majesty, grace, power, sweetness, bigness, generosity, graciousness, true, loving, lovely, admirable, trusting nature is incomparable to no one. The more we appreciate these unique attributes of God the more we can live life from His perspective because in Him we live, move and have our being (Acts 17:28). The real power for godly living and true praise comes from our All-Knowing God. God is all powerful and there is none greater than the Almighty. Praise God for His presence with us now and His promise of eternal life (Psalm 73:25-28). "For the kingdom is the Lord's, and He rules over the nations" (Psalm 22:28).

The Everlasting, Infallible, Magnificient and Eternal Father

Our Papa calls Himself the I Am that I Am (Exodus 3:14). This name of Our Father who is totally independent of His Creation and who was and is and will continue to be, is eternal. His Name shall endure forever and continue as long as the sun shines (Psalm 72:17). Time has no limit for Him. God who is holy, inhabits eternity (Isaiah 57:15). He is the God of eternal present. He is the eternal provider He is Alpha and Omega: The First and the Last. The Beginning and the End (Revelation 21:6). God was before everything and He will still be here after everything is gone. He is our everlasting Father. He is the God whose beginning we do not know and whose end we will not comprehend. He is self-existent and self-dependent. He is eternal. Underneath us are His everlasting arms (Deuteronomy 33:27). He will neither leave us nor forsake us (Deuteronomy 31:6&8).

Our earthly father eventually leaves us. But our eternal Heavenly Father is always present with us. And Our Father gives us an everlasting consolation (2 Thessalonians 2:16). This should give us hope and make us sing for joy. The eternal values of our Father give us glimpses into His unmatchable power, strength and allow us to look at the fact that our God is not hindered by time. This timelessness should make us think deeply about His unconditional love and incomprehensible protection for us as His children. We should marvel at His eternal nature and approach Him with awe, respect, adoration, devotion and reverence. But understand one thing as the Word says, eternal values are what really count so seek first the kingdom of God (Matthew 6:33). So, what you think about God matters in how you relate to Him and how you plan your life. A.W.Tozer in "The Knowledge of the Holy," reiterated that the most important thing about us is what we think about God. Who is God to us?

Few of us have let our hearts gaze in wonder at the I AM (that I AM), the self-existent Self, back of which no creature can think. Such thoughts are too painful for us. We prefer to think where it will do more good—about how to make a better mousetrap, for instance, or how to make two blades of grass grow where one grew before. And for this we are now paying a too heavy price in the secularization of our religion, and the decay of our inner lives (p.34).

It is important for us to comprehend God for who He is. Our Heavenly Father who will be there for us in all circumstances that life throws at us and for all occasions. The everlasting, infallible, magnificient and eternal Father. So, take time every day to think about your Heavenly Papa who is dancing and singing over you now. God who is sovereign, supreme, unchanging and undeniably great is our Rock, our Solid and Immovable Foundation. He is the Sustainer, the Ruler of the world, who is the limitless God of possibilities who reveals all hideous thoughts. This competent and reliable Father is our sure, unshakeable Tower. Our Papa is mightier than all. "The Lord is king! He is robed in majesty. Indeed, the Lord is robed in majesty and armed with strength. The world stands firm and cannot be shaken" (Psalm 93:1). It is penned in verse 4 of Psalm 93 that God is "mightier than the thunders of many waters, mightier than the waves of the sea, the Lord on high is mighty." The Psalmist continued to say that God's throne has stood from time immemorial and that Our Father is from everlasting past (Psalm 93:2).

He is the God who is able through His mighty and everlasting power to work within us to accomplish infinitely more than we might ask or think or even imagine (Ephesians 3:10). The seas and oceans obey His commands (Psalm 114). Chek Phang Hia of Our Daily Bread

Ministries advised us to never measure God's unlimited power by our limited expectations. We should also know that Our Papa has loved us with an everlasting love (Jeremiah 31:3). And that everything is possible for a limitless God!Our God is sovereign and Supreme (Psalm 86). God's love is eternal, infallible and unfazed.

God! Our relational Father

We perceive God the Father through God the Son and God the Son introduces us to God the Holy Spirit. They are Three-In-One: The Trinity. We are introduced to this fact in Genesis 1 verse 26, where God was introduced to us as a Community. God called on to the Trinity and reiterated: "Let Us (the Three of Us) make man in our image according to Our likeness" (Genesis 1:26). God shows us that "God" "is a community--- a community of three persons who relate to one another in perfect harmony. No quarrels, no arguments, no tensions. The Father loves the Son and gives Him everything (John 3:35). The Son always does that which pleases the Father (John 8:29). The Spirit takes the things of the Son and shows them to us (John 16:15).

We learn from the Trinity that relationship is the essence of reality and therefore the essence of our existence" (God in His own Community, Every Day With Jesus, February 14, 2018). Broughton Knox pointed out that, "when you touch the heart of the universe, you touch a God who relates. There is warmth, not just wonder, at the heart of the Trinity---the warmth of interpersonal relation-ships." God is a relational God ! Heavenly Father, help us to pursue a relationship with every part of who You are in Jesus' Name Amen. God Let us be in awe and reverence for God the Father, God the Son and God the Holy Spirit Amen. Heavenly Father is our Guide and

Guard, God the Son is our friend, brother and confidant. God the Son is called Wonderful, Counselor, Mighty God, Everlasting Father and Prince of Peace (Isaiah 9:6) and Immanuel (Isaiah 7:14; Matthew 1:23). Jesus Christ's birth in history depicts to us the One who is born into the world but Who is not from the world. Jesus came into history from the outside (Oswald Chambers) from God the Father. His birth was an advent---the appearance of God in human form. The Highest and Holiest coming to man in humility. God the Father was so elated by Jesus that He let the world know that "He is His beloved Son in whom He is well pleased" at His baptism (Matthew 3:17).

While God the Holy Spirit is our Director. Jesus promised that He will ask God to send the Comforter, Advocate, Intercessor, Strengthener, Counselor and Standby which is the Holy Spirit to His disciples and to us new believers to be with us and direct us in our Christian walk (John 14:16, 26; John 15:26). This promise has held true for all of us today because the Holy Spirit continues to lead and direct us as we faithfully walk the Christian walk. We love you Lord our triune Father. We defer to You for all the trials, successes and tribulations on our journey here.

The God of more than enough !

As I wrote above under the names that we call God, He is El Shaddai: The All-Sufficient Father (Psalm 91:1). That is the God who is more than enough. He was all sufficient for Abraham, for Moses and the children of Israel at the mouth of the Red Sea (Exodus 14), for Joshua when the sun and moon stood still (Joshua 10:13) and throughout his advent into the promised land, for Joseph, Daniel, David, Solomon and our fore-parents of faith who were leaders, judges, prophets, priests, queen and kings.

The God of more than enough is the Almighty God--- the All-Sufficient Father who sent ravens to feed Elijah and showcased His unlimited power when Elijah prayed on Mount Carmel and the fire of God consumed the sacrifice he made. Eventually, the power of God aids him in the defeat of the prophets of Baal (1 Kings 18:17-40). Our Unlimited Father is the I AM that I AM. He is a God who is and not a God who was. He is a God who still reigns today. And what He has done for others, He will do for you because His power still prevails today. Trust in the El Shaddai and it shall be well with you. And His yoke is easy His burden is light (Matthew 11:30). We found it so, we find it so. He leads us by day and by night where living waters flow. Our God is our protector and comforter. A God who listens to us when we call on Him. A God who shows us mercy and compassion when we are in despair and have no hope left. A God who gives us strength when we are tired. He is our only hope and salvation comes from Him through Our Lord Jesus Christ. And this our God shall supply all our needs according to His riches in Christ Jesus (Philippians 4:19). I end this section with the song: "More than enough for us."

> You hold my every moment
> You calm my raging seas
> You walk with me through fire
> You heal all my disease
> I trust in You, I trust in You
> I believe You're my healer
> I believe You are all I need
> I believe You're my portion
> I believe You're more than enough for me
> Jesus You're all I need

You hold my very moment

You calm my raging seas

You walk with me through fire

And heal all my disease

I trust in You, Lord I trust in You

I believe You're my healer

I believe You are all I need

I believe You're my portion

I believe You're more than enough for me

Jesus You're all I need

Nothing is impossible for You

Nothing is impossible

Nothing is impossible for You

You hold my world in Your hands

Nothing is impossible for You

Nothing is impossible

Nothing is impossible for You

You hold my world in Your hands

I believe You're my healer

I believe You are all I need

Jesus

I believe You're my portion

I believe You're more than enough for me

Yes Jesus You're all I need

You're more than enough for me, yeah

Jesus You're all I need

More than enough for me

Source: Musixmatch

Songwriters: Michael Jonathan Guglielmucci

Healer lyrics © Lilly Mack Music, M3m Music, Planet Shakers Ministries International Inc.

God the Father wants to have a relationship with you

Abba Father, the Creator of the Universe and your Creator wants to have a personal relationship with you. Will you abide with Him? He is calling you to come. Will you heed His call and be counted worthy as one of His? If you heed His call you shall remain in Him as the grape remains in the vine (John 15). You shall be rooted in the Almighty because He that is planted in the Almighty shall not be moved. The love of God is already ours when we accept Jesus Christ as our Savior. Jesus is enough for us (Philippians 4:19). God gave us the right to become children of the King (John 1:12). God considers each of us important enough to represent Him here on earth after we accept Jesus and also one day reign with Him (2 Timothy 2:11-13). Yes, we have a part to play in God's Kingdom (John 1:12). Jesus showed us how much we are loved (John 3:14-17) by allowing us to spit on him, mock Him, and crucify Him: The Creator of the Universe.

The Word asks in Romans 8 verse 35 that: "Who shall separate us from the love of Christ? Shall tribulation, or distress, or persecution, or famine, or nakedness, or peril, or sword?" Accept Jesus Christ as your Savior and hold on fast to Jesus and pray that you do not let anything separate you from His love. Always tell yourself: "I have set the Lord always before me; Because He is at my right hand I shall not be moved" (Psalm 16:8). As apple of God's eye, He has also hidden you under the shadow of His Wings (Psalms 17:8).

Because God is also your rock and strength and your fortress and deliverer in Him you should trust. So, if you trust in Him, He will keep you securely in His Arms and nothing can separate you from Him. You are saying to yourself. You don't know what I am going through. What is ailing you? What is the mountain standing before you? (Zechariah 4:7). God has given you the strength to scale it if you rely totally in Him. When you speak to your mountain after you have made Him your Lord and Savior, it shall be removed by faith (Mark 11: 23-24), because as Paul said, nothing, NOTHING can separate you from the love of Jesus Christ. If you love God with all your heart and lean not on your understanding you are so so secure in the palm of His Hand and safe in the might of His Hands (Psalm 89:13). No evil can come near you or your household. The only thing you need to do is put your whole trust in the Lord and rest securely in His everlasting Arms because the eternal God who is your refuge and fortress wants to have a relationship with you and underneath you are His everlasting arms (Deuteronomy 33:27).

We are hidden with Christ in His glory (2 Corinthians 3:18). When we belong to God, we are solely His and no one can have us (Ephesians 2:10 & 4:12). No one can steal us out of His Hand. Are you His? If not yet, say your prayers of repentance now and accept Jesus Christ into your heart as your Lord and Savior. He is waiting for you and you can be like me standing solid on the Rock of our Salvation. And once you are His, He will be a wall of fire all around you and He will be your Glory (Zechariah 2:5). For Our God is all consuming fire (Hebrews 12:29). So, what is the problem you are going through. Bring it to the cross after you have established a relationship with your Father. Lay it down and don't let it separate you from Christ's love. God loved us so much that He sent His Son to shed His blood for us. His watchful eyes are constantly following us everywhere we

MARY OLUFUNMILAYO ADEKSON

go because of His unconditional LOVE for us. He sits on the throne advocating and praying for us.

Yes, you are an important person to God Almighty: The Creator of the Universe. And because of this, His protective Hand shields you and the precious Blood of Jesus Christ covers you and your household. So be assured nothing can separate you from His love once you recognize and accept Him as Lord. Just hold on tight by reading the Word of God, Praying, Praising and abiding in His will, showing gratitude to Him and through your service to others. Only in the Lord who is near the broken hearted, can we truly find true love, peace, safety, rest, security and trust. He is the rock whose presence we can always depend on (Deuteronomy 32:4; Psalm 34:15).

Take Father God seriously

As I have portrayed in the chapters before this, God our Father is supreme. He is our all in all. Nobody can compare to Him or compete with Him. He created our Universe and the world's diverse people from all nations (Revelation 5:9) and He keeps the Universe in place securely. So, listen to God the Father as the One in authority. Because great is the Lord, and greatly to be praised, and He is to be held in awe above all gods (1 Chronicles 16:25).

For the Lord your God is God of gods, and Lord of lords, the great God, mighty and awesome, who shows no partiality and accepts no bribes (Deuteronomy 10:17). He is clothed with splendor and majesty (Psalm 104:1). Take Him and His promises seriously. When I remember His promises, I shout Halleluia. When I remember His promises, I shout Halleluia. Respect Him. Stand in awe of Him. Love Him. Defer to Him in all cases about your life and your well-being. Be humble before Him (James 4:6). Lord, give us a spirit that is humble and responsive to You (Psalm 149:4; Psalm 138:6; James 4:6 &10; Micah 6:8; Isaiah 66:2; Proverbs 3:34) Amen. Living with integrity through humility allows us to submit unreservedly to God and look at following His plans for our lives (James 4:8). We therefore humbly become friends of God not friends of the world (James 3:15 & 17; 4:4). This humble attitude makes us wise and victorious over Satan and its cohorts (James 4:7).

Be meek. Jesus said "blessed are the meek for they shall inherit the earth" (Matthew 5:5). The meek possess God's strength with complete submission to His will. They have the inner convictions and confidence that help them have power to do His will. They are not weak. They possess God's transforming power to assist others and do the bidding of God. They have God's strength under control. And do not grumble. Grumbling displeases the Lord (Numbers 11:1; 14:2). Do not complain.

Count your blessings because God has blessed us with all spiritual blessings (Ephesians 1:3). Name these blessings one by one. And it will surprise you what the Lord has done. "And whatever you do, do it heartily as to the Lord and not for men, knowing that from the Lord you will receive the reward of the inheritance for you serve the Lord Christ" (Colossians 3:23-24). Take His Word seriously. Thy Word have I hidden in my heart that I might not sin against you (Psalm 119:11). Be serious with Him. Do not be wise in your own eyes. Be pleasing to God (2 Corinthians 5:9).

Don't play God about events in your life or that of others. Always remember that He has the whole world in His Hands every second of the day. Yes, believe it that God has the whole world in His Hands. He has the whole wide world in His Hands. He is the Alpha and Omega. God is majestic in all the earth (Psalm 8). God has you inscribed in the palms of His Hands as the apple of His eye (Psalm 17:8). The eternal God is your refuge and underneath you are His everlasting arms (Deuteronomy 33:27). And He will neither leave nor forsake you (Deuteronomy 31:6 & 8).

Trust God for who He is, not for the blessings He bestows on you. If we trust Him for who He is like Job did, we will say like Job said that, "God is wise in heart and mighty in strength" (Job 9:4). When we trust Him for who He is, He unreservedly bestows His blessings on us without reservation like He did for Job at the end of his trials and tribulations. The Preacher, whom many believe was Solomon, spoke of the frustrations and disappointments of life (Ecclesiastes 1:1). He concludes that the answer to this meaninglessness is to look beyond this world 'under the sun' (Ecclesiastes 1:3) and remember our Creator (Ecclesiastes 12:1) who is the only source of true meaning in this life and who is the center of our lives (Ecclesiastes 3:11 & 1-14).

I stand in awe of you !

Let us end this section on embracing and acknowledging our Papa as a competent and reliable Father, with Mark Altrogge's powerful song about our Papa.

> You are beautiful beyond description
> Too marvelous for words
> Too wonderful for comprehension
> Like nothing ever seen or heard
> Who can grasp your infinite wisdom?
> Who can fathom the depths of your love?
> You are beautiful beyond description

Majesty enthroned above

And I stand, I stand in awe of you

I stand I stand in awe of you

Holy God to whom all praises due

I stand in awe of you.

(Mark Altrogge, 1987)

This song points to the infinite and eternal nature of our incomprehensible, beautiful, wonderful and incomparable Father. Nobody can grasp our Papa's infinite wisdom or fathom the depths of His unconditional love to us. God is truly magnificent and bigger than what we can think or envisage. We should therefore stand in wonder, admiration and marvel at His love with outstretched arms and praises and gratitude with awe-filling respect to our Competent and Reliable Father. The All-Knowing God who takes excellent care of us every day. We should marvel at out Father's GREATNESS and HOLINESS with utmost humility. Give God your all. Thanksgiving is an important part of true worship to our Creator. Offer to God thanksgiving and pay your vows to the Most High. Call upon Him on the day of trouble and He will deliver us and give us the grace to glorify His Name (Psalm 50:14-15). The essence and core of salvation is Thanksgiving. So, give your all to the Mighty One. So, magnanimously give God everything because He owns everything (Psalm 50:10). God who is excellent and great and who can be compared to no one, owns us and all we have. Offer to God sacrifice of praise, let the fruits of your lips openly profess His Name (Hebrews 13:15).

Have a heart that yearns for the Lord your Father

What does the Holy Bible say about the heart of man?

THE AMAZING HEART WHICH beats 100,000 times a day [65-70 times a minute] with no time off for rest to get most of us through about seventy years or more, is amazingly made by God to sustain our inner well-being. As Psalm 73 verse 26 echoes, God is the strength of our heart and our portion forever. God through His infinite power sustains and keeps our hearts pure, strong, holy and transformed. What we allow into our spiritual hearts is as important what transpires in our physical hearts.

The Lord said to Samuel, "do not consider his appearance or his height, for I have rejected him. The Lord does not look at the things man looks at. Man looks at the outward appearance, but the Lord looks at the heart" (1 Samuel 16:7). This cogent point and realization say a lot about what God is thinking regarding our hearts. This should teach us not to judge the book by its cover. Not to judge individuals according to their outward appearance. For God knows our hearts and He will bring every thought and action into judgement because we reap what we sow (Ecclesiastes 12:14; Galatians 6:7; 1 Samuel 16:7; Proverbs 10:9; Isaiah 55:8-9; Matthew 12:34-37; Colossians 4:6). "The heart is deceitful above all else and desperately wicked. Who can know it?" (Jeremiah 17:9). One thing that is certain is that, we as human beings cannot hide what is in our hearts from God. God knows our hearts and all our intentions. Most people hide what is in their hearts from other human beings. But God knows our heart. "For the righteous God probes the hearts and minds" ...... and "saves the upright in heart" (Psalm 7: 9-10). According to First Kings 8 verse 39, God is the only one who knows what is in human hearts. "I the Lord search the heart, I test the mind. Even to give every man (and woman) according to his (or her) ways. According to the fruit of his (or her) doings" (Jeremiah 17:10). Our Father repays everyone according to what is in their hearts. God sees the pride, the envy, the jealousy, coveteousness and more, that lay hidden in each person's heart. Solomon says: Keep your heart with all diligence for out of it flows the issues of life (Proverbs 4:23). What are the issues of life: emotions, plans, anxiety, lusts, joys, pains, sadness and much more. From our hearts flow love, bitterness, hatred, envy, anger to mention a few of the emotions we go through daily in life. Although David was referred to as a man after God's heart, he was as human as we all are.

In Hebrews 10 verses 15 to16, God promises to write His laws into our hearts. Proverbs 3 verse 5 reiterates that we should acknowledge the Lord in all our ways so that He shall direct our paths. Isaiah 29 verse 13 warns us to be closer to Him with our hearts and do not let our hearts be far from Him. Romans 10 verses 9 and 10 posits "that if you confess with your mouth the Lord Jesus and believe in your heart that God raised Him from the dead you will be saved. For with the heart one believes unto righteousness, and with the mouth confession is made unto salvation." Let your heart rest on the security and peace that only God can give. God clothes us in Jesus Christ's robe of righteousness obtained at the Cross at Calvary. Give the possession of your heart to the Almighty and you will never be the same again. You will be transformed. Those who have peace in their own hearts are able to share that with others. When we are not at peace with God, we are not at peace within ourselves and others (James 3:18). Internal turmoil results. When we find peace with God, a change takes place in our hearts and our lives and we become peaceable people. We become peacemakers, reconcilers. We reconcile people to God and to each other. This requires a lot of courage and work and the inspiration of the Holy Spirit. May God inspire and aid you and give you strength to be a peacemaker Amen (1 Corinthians 16:13). May Christ's peace be within our hearts (John 14:27) Amen.

The Bible is self-authenticating to us Christians. It speaks to us at our greatest depths. It reveals deep answers about God and life to us. It reveals the condition and needs of our hearts and equips us as God's servant (2 Timothy 3:16-17). Jesus our Savior fed upon the Word of God while He was here on earth. God reveals Himself to us through His Word. The Word purifies our hearts, opens our Spiritual eyes to see, and enables us to move closer to God (Psalm 119:16,18).

What corrupts the heart of man?

All human beings inherited the sin of our fore-father, Adam. This sin permeates to us through our relationship with the world, friends and acquaintances. David exclaimed in Psalm 116 verse 11 that "all men are liars." Some of the saints used by God all had a smeared badge to show that we have all fall short through sins. Simon Peter, the Rock and one of the Christian founding fathers denied Jesus three times under oath (Matthew 26:70-72) after assuring Jesus he will never disown Him (Mark 14:31). Paul messed up with his lips when he called God's High Priest a "white-washed wall" (Acts 23:3). He later withdrew and apologized a few moments later (Acts 23:5). Gideon doubted God (Judges 6:13) and Jonah said some words that could have tested God's patience in Jonah 4 verses 2 to 4. May God cleanse and purify us with the Holy ghost fire like He did with Isaiah in Isaiah 6 verses 6 to 7, and also in the Psalmist prayer in Psalm 141 verse 3 where he implores God to set a guard over his mouth so he can become pure and holy Amen. May God purify our hearts so we can daily have pure thoughts and act in holy and Christ-like and approved ways. Amen. Pain, anger and agony and hurt come from the way people relate to other people without love. This eventually leads to experiences of injustice, inequality, hurt and fear in the lives of so many people.

The things of this world are temporary. Most often what we can see corrupts the heart of man. We should not therefore "fix our eyes on what is seen but on what is unseen. For what is seen is temporary, but what is unseen is eternal" (2 Corinthians 4:18). Unseen things are intangible like patience, sensitivity, faith, goodness, perseverance, self-control and love to name a few (Galatians 5:22-23). We should remember that we are in the world but not of the world (John 17:14-15). Conform to the values of Jesus Christ (Romans 12:1-2; John 17:16).

Sin corrupts the heart of man. You might ask ? What is sin? Sin is any act that is against the laid-down law of God (Exodus 20). Your next question is: How do I identify sin? The Word of God is full of admonitions against sin. In Mark 7 verses 21 to 23 Jesus said, it is "what comes out of a man, that defiles a man. For from within, out of the heart of men, proceed evil thoughts, adulteries, fornications, murders, thefts, covetousness, wickedness, deceit, lewdness, an evil eye, blasphemy, pride, foolishness." And Galatians 5 verses 19 to 21 echoes these sins as well. All these evil things come from within and defile a man (or woman). If God call something evil it is evil no matter what the world says or is saying about it, Sin is sin. Run from it. It is poison of death that kills. Those that commits sin will get the consequences here on earth and end up in the lake of fire if they don't repent and put a stop to sin in their lives (Revelation 20:14). To steer away from sin, you must be very conversant with the Word of God and like Galatians 5 verse 16 says, walk in the Spirit and you shall not fulfill the lusts of the flesh. "The fruit of the Spirit is, love, joy, peace, long-suffering, kindness, goodness, faithfulness, gentleness, self-control" (Galatians 5 22). So, crucify your flesh with its passions and desires and put on Jesus Christ. Wear Him. And be blessed like the man or woman who walked not in the counsel of the ungodly but delights in the laws and Word of God (Psalm 1:1-3). You can be pure just as your Father in heaven is pure and holy. Draw on God's grace every time even before temptation or sin rear its head. You do this by watching and praying. Draw close to the Shepherd and the 'wolf' Satan: the enemy, and temptation will run away from you (James 4:8). Trust God and He will always lead you to do the right things that will glorify His Name. Lean on the Almighty God who created heaven and earth and who formed you and brought you here to fulfill His purpose.

Choose your words carefully and biblically and take responsibility for your thoughts and actions. Philippians 4 verse 8 says, "Finally brethren, whatever things are true, whatever things are noble, whatever things are just, whatever things are pure, whatever things are lovely, whatever things are of good report, if there be any virtue and if there be anything praiseworthy---meditate on these things." Your next question will be: "how can I separate myself from all the worldly things that can so easily attach themselves to me." Repent, immerse yourself in The Word of God and see what the Word says about sin and how to flee from the devil and its cohorts who entices you to sin (James 4:7). Pray. Praise. Be on your guard for small and big sins and also guard your hearts, your eyes, your soul, mind and your words. Be holy and pure as your Heavenly Father and Jesus are holy. Expose yourself to the Holy Spirit. Let Him direct your paths and your thoughts and alertly heed His warnings. Do not grieve the Holy Spirit. Place a barricade between you and sin. Say to yourself every time there is temptation as it will rear its head, that, "I am not going there". I am going to be on the Lord's side and commit no sin. And when you sin as we are all human and prone to do, be ready to repent like David did (Psalms 32 & 51) and do not go back to commit self-defeating and self-destructive sins anymore. Then, like David you can become a woman or a man after God's heart. Therefore, as Songwriter Charlie Hall wrote a song rendered by Chris Tomlin which praises: "So, give us clean hands and give us pure hearts. Let us not lift our souls to another. Oh God let us be a generation that seeks, who seeks Your face Oh God of Jacob." May the Holy Spirit continue to guide, guard us and lead us to live a sinless life so we can reign with Him after our work here is done Amen.

What can change and free man's heart?

God will free you morally, emotionally, psychologically and spiritually (Psalm 107:13-14; John 8:36; Jeremiah 29:13; 1 Peter 5:7; John 6:51; Luke 4:18; Matthew 5:3-16). Take time to ruminate and meditate on God's Word. Reflect on it until you understand what it is saying to you and how God is relaying its meaning for your life and circumstance. Understand how to apply it to your life because knowledge without application is useless. You gain freedom and feed your heart and mind by feeding daily on the Word of God and at the same time applying what you learn to your present situation. "I have hidden your Word in my heart, that I might not sin against You" (Psalm 119:11 & 117). "God, may your Word be our source for daily strength, encouragement, comfort when we're in pain, hope when we're facing despair, guidance when we've lost our way, and everlasting love that only comes from you" (Bill Crowder, Our Daily Bread Ministries). It is through immersing ourselves in and meditating in the Word of God, focusing on the Lord's commands, constant prayer and communicating with Almighty Father that we can be delivered and our hearts set free from worldly enticements that can make our heart wander and fall into sin. When you meditate on the Word of God you will be like a man or woman who builds his or her house on a rock and when the turbulence of worldly problems and adversity engulfs her or him, he or she will stand firm (Matthew 7: 24-27).

Your total dependence should be on God after you have accepted Jesus Christ as your Savior. C. S Lewis reiterated that, "a real Person, Christ ...... is doing things to you.....gradually turning you permanently into....a new little Christ, a being which....shares in His power, joy, knowledge and eternity." God is always working in our hearts if we turn it to Him. He is the only one that makes a heart of stone becomes a heart of flesh (Ezekiel 36:26; 11:19; Jeremiah 31:33; Hebrews 8:10). The bottom line is that we need to turn our hearts to God for spiritual surgery to take place in our hearts, this thereby leads to transformation of our lives. Holy Spirit cleans away the clouds of sin and darkness from our hearts, so we are able to see God more clearly. Paul said that this gives us a pure heart (1 Timothy 1:5) and gives us pure conscience (1 Timothy 3:9). He implored us to call on the Lord out of a pure heart (2 Timothy 2:22). Jesus said blessed are the pure in heart for they shall see God (Matthew 5:8). Paul reiterated further that we should put on the Lord Jesus Christ and make no provision for the flesh and so we do not fulfill its lusts (Romans 13:14). Solomon concluded that a man or a woman cannot find the true essential joy of his or her life anywhere else but in her or his relationship to God (Ecclesiastes 12:13).

As born-again Christians, the Holy Spirit cleans our hearts if we allow Him to. That is, if we listen to Him. He clears away the garbage in our hearts and replaces them with kindness, compassion, love and the fruit of the Spirit (Galatians 5:22-23). He is there in our hearts to correct any unclean situation, not to condemn us. He solemnly chastises us and replaces what is undesirable with desirable Godly attributes. So, ask God to give you a pure heart that is undivided, a heart that seeks to draw close to God and thereby make God its chief goal (Psalm 86:11). A heart that is sincere and single but not double minded (James 1:7-8). A heart that is whole and free from impurity and defilement (Revelation 21:27). A heart that will prepare us to see God. Jesus came to give us life and that life in abundance (John 10:10). When you immerse yourself in the Word and pray and let the Holy Spirit be your Director, your heart will be pure.

You need to eat the Word: The Spiritual food every day in order to have a pure and Godly heart (Jeremiah 15:16). Holy Spirit guides, cleanses and delivers you daily from wicked thoughts and deeds. When we are weary and think we cannot go on anymore,

Jesus proclaims that He will give us rest (Matthew 11:28). When we think that nobody cares, Jesus professes His love for us (John 15:12-13). God's Hand guides us when we cannot figure out how things will turn out for us (Psalm 48:14). God's Hand of forgiveness finds us out when we need to be forgiven (1 John 1:9). Jesus Christ professed that we should love our neighbors as ourselves (Matthew 22:36-40; Mark 12:30-31). William Wordsworth reiterated that "that best portion of a good man's (or woman's) life/(are) (her or) his little, nameless, unremembered acts/of kindness and of love."

Christ showed us how to love one another through His actions while on earth. He still loves us as both God the Father and God the Holy Spirit do. Jesus extended mercy to all. The One who held all power surrendered every bit of it for the sake of love. God gave us His Son because of love. For God so love the world that He gave us His only Son, so we do not perish, but have everlasting life (John 3:16). God and Jesus want you to do the same for others (Matthew 5:7). Our relationship with God should always cause us to extend mercy to all in need. Love is not walking past those who are hurting or in pain. We should show mercy to those in pain and those who are hurting. How can we do this? How can our heart bleed with love towards others? By loving Jesus Christ. By having a close relationship with our Father and adhering to and doing what the Word says. Real change comes through hearts that are transformed by Jesus Christ and the Word of God (2 Timothy 3:16-17) and being conformed to the image of Jesus Christ (Romans 8:29; 1 John 3:2; Ephesians 4:24). We are all made in God's image (Genesis 1:27).

Loving our neighbors as ourselves (Matthew 22:34-40; Mark 12:30-31) as well as loving God will make us be like the Good Samaritan who showed mercy to a Jew even though the Jews disliked him and regarded him as an enemy (Luke 10:30-37). As we will all stand together as a nation, tribe and from every tongue to worship Our Father (Revelation 7:9), let us start practicing love for others now. Someone who has a loving and merciful heart sees beyond ethnic, cultural or religious differences and look beyond fear, disrespect, hatred, and suspicion that has prevailed within the society for centuries. Be like the Good Samaritan by casting away fear and distrust from your heart today (Ephesians 2:13-14). Embrace love, humility and compassion. Let no arrogance prevail within your heart. Let go of 'Me-First' attitude. Have mercy towards everyone regardless of the color of their skin or where they come from. Consider how your words, actions and attitudes impact other people. Does your word lift up people or tear them apart?

Your words come from what is in your heart. Make a difference in somebody's life daily through your words, actions and attitudes. Have a heart of gratitude to God and your fellow human beings. Value your fellow sojourners on your life's journey here by having a positive attitude that stems from a pure heart. You can do this through respect for others: those like you and those different from you. Search your heart and ask God to search you and see if there is any wicked way within you (Psalm 139:23-24). God will lead you into everlasting way. Lord, let your will find a lodging place in our hearts in Jesus' Name Amen.

See others. Support others. Love others. Be a source of healing for your fellow men and women. Listen and share their pains, frustration, and grief. When you have the heart of God, you let the splendor of love, joy, peace, patience, kindness, compassion, comfort, faithfulness and self-control that emanates from God shine through you to those around you (Matthew 5:16). Turn to God by finding a quiet place that is close to the heart of God to have this kind of heart. Examine your deeper self by looking into what is in your heart. How well and deep in Jesus Christ are you growing? (2 Peter 3:10-18; 1 Peter 2:1-2; 2 Peter 1:2-8). Do not give God the leftover of your time, energy, and heart. Give God the best of all you have got. Put God first (Isaiah 40:31; Proverbs 3:9-10). As we walk closer with Jesus and the Lord, we start to know more about the Lord and ourselves. And as Moses "found grace in (God's) sight and He knew Moses by name (Exodus 33:17), we will also find favor and grace from Our Father. Our inner doubts and sins are exposed.

Undesirable things within our hearts are revealed and we can start working on them to become whole as God's blood-bought child. We will know more about our inner motives and understand why we behave in the way we behave. Don't give in to Satan through doubts, lies, shock, negative feelings and emotions, rely on truth (John 8:31-32 & 44). Stand your ground with Jesus Christ as your High Priest and Risen Savior.

Peter 'the Great Fisherman' evolve from an impulsive, proud, outspoken, loud-mouthed, coward who denied his Lord three times, to become the greatest apostle and a good leader after Jesus' Resurrection (Luke 5:8, 1-11; John 1:41; Matthew 14:22-33; 26:34; 16:18; John 21:17; Acts 2:14-41). And how about Saul, who later became Paul after his conversion on the way to Damascus (Acts 9:1-19). Paul's heart and life were transformed by Jesus (Acts 9:17-18). The man who plotted to kill Christians became one of the most powerful witnesses of the gospel of Jesus Christ in history. God can do this to us too if we open our hearts to Him because Peter and Paul were human like all of us. The Lord Jesus Christ allowed Peter to go deep into himself and thereby exposed his deeper love for Him. As a result of this Peter was able to be the catalyst for 3,000 souls at Pentecost to be welcomed into God's Kingdom (Acts 2: 14-41). Our Lord Jesus Christ looked into Peter and Paul's hearts and foresaw men they would eventually become: You are Simon, son of John and you will be called Cephas (John 1:42, 35-42). "You will suffer a lot for my sake" says the Lord to Saul (Acts 9:16). And you Peter will become a Rock upon which I will build my church Jesus said (Matthew 16:16-19). This is what God can do to us through redeeming our hearts if we let Him in. Jesus is saying to you now: you are (Insert your name here.....) and you will become my vessel. "Jesus takes us as we are and makes us what we should be" (David H. Roper, Our Daily Bread Ministries).

So, stay focused on God and let God search your hearts and cleanse you (Psalm 51:7). Because God reveals the sins in our lives so we can be healed and become whole (Psalm 25:4). Pray to God and go to the Cross for your redemption so He can become your priest (Hebrews 7:25). Let God examine your heart (Psalm 26:1-3; Proverbs 17:3; Isaiah 1:10-17; Psalm 139:17-24). May God reveal us to ourselves as we pursue Him with genuine hearts. Amen. May He use us to advance His Kingdom here on earth. Amen. May God remake us to be a woman and man after God's own heart like David (1 Samuel 13:14) and make us become closer to God like Moses so we can also perceive His glory (Exodus 33:18). Amen.

Because you are God's child, your life will go on well with your love and respect for your Father who gave you life and gave you the opportunity to work for Him as His witness here on earth. We can be sidetracked by everything that we own here on earth and thereby hold on tightly to them. Let us remember one wise thing: we are just stewards of all we own. Have you ever thought about having a heart of total and perfect surrender to God? It's easier said than done. Some people scheme, lie, cheat, pretend, connive, steal and do other things to accumulate wealth and fail to surrender their hearts to the One who gives them the power to get the wealth in the first place. Have you ever seen any dead person who takes anything with them when it's their time for them to answer the last call in death? When you die you are going to go to God naked as you come here in the first place even if they robe you in gold. The gold and all you are robed in will be consumed by ants and maggots. Do not get me wrong, there is nothing wrong with having wealth. The love and obsession with money and wealth will make you lose the will to surrender your heart to the Almighty and lose heaven and be doomed in eternity. So, surrender your heart to God. Because Jesus Christ died for us while we were yet sinners (Romans 5:5). Do not make material things your gods or idols and do not love the world and the things that are in the world (1 John 2:15-17). For the love of money (and even the love of material things) is the root of all evil (1 Timothy 6:10). As Jesus encouraged us in Matthew 16 verse 24: If you want to be God's disciple, you must take up your cross and follow Jesus in full and total surrender. David's total surrender allowed him to courageously conquer and kill Goliath with nothing but five smooth stones and a sling. When you heart is totally attuned and surrendered to God, no earthly thing will be of more value to you than serving and loving God and having a close relationship with Him. Total heart surrender allowed Moses to shun being called Pharaoh daughter's son and instead allowed him to embrace his Hebrew heritage. This attitude of total and perfect surrender made Moses become a close friend of God that he even asked God to show him His glory (Exodus 33:17-23). Total surrender made Paul to abandon his upscale background and instead become a witness of Our Lord Jesus Christ to the gentiles. Total and perfect surrender allowed Daniel to refuse to eat meat scarified to idols (Daniel 1:7-8). We can say this about Joseph, Noah, Shadrach, Meshach and Abednego, and Esther who, although a queen, identified as a Jew even if this identification could have resulted in death (Esther 4:15-16).

If you want to be a man or woman after God's heart like David, give your all to God including your **whole** heart. Serve Him without any reservation. And my dear, never worship man made gods. As I said earlier, do not love the world for whosoever loves the world the love of the Father is not in her or him (1 John 2:15). So, surrender your **ALL** to God in your life. Give God the key to your heart and He will give you a heart of flesh instead of a heart of stone and put His Spirit into you (Ezekiel 36:26-27). Follow God. Be a friend of God. Believe Him. Respect Him. And do not go back to the world like the rich young ruler in Luke 18. Enjoy life here with God, holding loosely to worldly things and valuables and happily spend eternity with your Papa. Make your life to become a testimony for God. Jesus' words in Matthew 6 verse 33 that admonishes us to seek the kingdom of God and His righteousness first and let God add all those other things of life to our lives should be the paramount basis of our lives. And believe me He will add them if you are faithful. You will enjoy your life with Him wholly here and thereafter spend eternity with Him. Shout Halleluia ! May God give us hearts totally surrendered to Him. Amen. God says: "I will give you a new heart and put a new spirit within you. God says, I will take the heart of stone out of your flesh and give you a heart of flesh. I will put My Spirit within you and cause you to walk in my statutes, and you will keep my judgements and do them" (Ezekiel 36:26-27; Jeremiah 31:33; Hebrews 8:10; 10:16; Romans 11:27). These promises are for you. Claim them and pray that God bring them to pass in your life. May God give all of us clean, holy and loving hearts. Amen.

Cherish self-control and self-discipline in your daily life and confront your emotions in front of God daily as you interact with people. God demand exclusive, undivided, wholehearted, loving attention and obedience with allegiance and devotion from us every day. Jesus informed us that the greatest, first and most important commandment is to love God with our total and whole being (Matthew 22:37). Moses also entreated the Israelites to love God in Deuteronomy 6 verse 5. Solomon reiterated in Ecclesiastes 12 verse 13 that fearing God and keeping the commandments is the ultimate basis of our faith as God's child and this is the conclusion of the matter. So, embrace God and you will never be the same again and walk within your house with a perfect heart (Psalm 101:2). May God let us live with a heart that is "hidden in Christ" (Colossians 3:3) Amen.

So, what's in your heart? And What are you thinking?

Our problems stems from what are in our hearts. Yes, what we are thinking. Jesus knows what we are thinking before we say it (Matthew 15:1-2; 7-8; Isaiah 29:13; Matthew 15:18-19; Proverbs 16:2, 21& 23; Jeremiah 17:5-10). The Lord knows our thoughts (Psalm 94:11). Our true nature will reveal itself in our words. For out of the heart the mouth speaks (Matthew 12:34). "The mouth speaks what the heart is full of," and Jesus pointed out that "a good (woman or) man speaks out of the good stored up in (her or) his heart, and an evil man (woman) speaks out of the evil stored up in her or his heart" (Luke 6:45). It is our hearts not just our words that need to come under control through the help of our Father who has the ultimate power to help us. Because our words reveal what is in our hearts. Turn around and move toward God's promises with hope firmly planted in your heart. Replace old thoughts with empowering truth from God's Word that will empower and strengthen you for a renewed way of living. Turn around and move forward with God who has no hint of condemnation towards you (Psalm 32:8; 25:12). Psalm 36 verses 1 to 4 summarizes the wickedness that hides in man's heart. We should heed the Word of God as Psalm 37 reveals, so we do not come to judgement. And James 3 verses 17 to 18 resonates that our hearts should reveal the life-changing Spirit of Jesus Christ in our daily living and interactions. As a man or woman thinks, so is he or her (Proverbs 23:7). Roxanne Robbins of Our Daily Bread Ministries reiterated that, "If our hearts are full of bitterness or hatred, broken relationships and isolation will follow. (And) if our hearts are full of love, compassion, and gratitude, we'll tend to have healthy, edifying relationships." Have you ever heard the saying: As you think so you are? (Proverbs 23:7). J. Oswald Sanders reiterated that, "the mind of man (or woman) is the battleground on which every moral and spiritual battle is fought" (2 Corinthians 10:5).

It is estimated that you think between 60,000 to 80,000 thoughts a day. That is 2,500 thoughts an hour and 42 thoughts a minute. So, what's in your heart my dear sister and brother? May God the Comforter shed abroad the love of God in our hearts and birth forth the fruit of love, joy, peace, long-suffering, kindness, good-ness, faithfulness, meekness, temperance, grace, mercy, purity, and Godly compassion, power and righteousness into our lives through our thoughts and actions. Amen. You cannot overcome negative and wrong thoughts by your self-effort but you can do it through faith in Jesus Christ and immersing yourself in the Word of God daily so you can become an image of the invincible God (Psalm 141:8; John 3:16; Colossians 1:15) and through prayer and heeding the nudgings of the Holy Spirit, listening to Godly music and messages, singing praise songs to the Lord. Fill your mind with the Word of God and focus on the Lord's commands, promises and goodness. And do not forget to adhere to and meditate on all the things that are true, noble, just, pure, lovely and of good report (Philippians 4:8). These will make you become like God's Son. What comes out of a man? (Mark 7:21-23). Anne Cetas of Our Daily Bread Ministries implored us to "let no thoughts linger in your mind that you would be ashamed to let out of your mouth." When you get up in the morning, pray that the words of your mouth and the meditations of your heart become accept-able and pleasing to the Lord your rock and redeemer (Psalm 19:14; 119:117). So, if your heart is not right now, the spirit within you will nudge you. Repent for the Lord is good. This was why Jesus came. To redeem us and cleanse us from our sins. This is the day of repen-tance. Today is the day of salvation. Be cleansed today God's joy.

"For the weapons of our warfare are not carnal but mighty in God for pulling down strongholds. Casting down arguments and every high thing that exalts itself against the knowledge of God, bringing every thought into captivity in the obedience of Christ" (2 Corinthians 10:4-5). Your thoughts are supposed to be your great ally as a follower of Jesus Christ. Stop berating yourself. What you think matters. Think of yourself and see yourself as Jesus Christ and God do. Take all negative thoughts captive and let these thoughts bow to the obedience of Jesus Christ. Destroy lies that constantly come to your mind and remember who you are in Christ. Wrestling and re-placing negative self-talk with positive ones will bring all hateful and un-Christlike thoughts captive. War with them by using the Word of God, prayer and praise as I pointed out earlier. Holy Spirit will come to your aid as you pray and strive to keep all negative thoughts captive. God who has redeemed you, and bought you with the pre-cious blood of Jesus, will make you succeed in doing this (Ephesians 1:5-6). Let the devil know you are God's jewel and that you and your thoughts are God's possession. See yourself as an overcomer be-cause you are more than conquerors through Christ who redeemed you (Romans 8:37). Thank God for His blessings, love, grace, mercy, goodness, peace, lovingkindness, hope, protection, provision, faith, and much more. God is excellent all the time and He leads us in His ways. God is the real Father. He sees all things and reveals all hid-eous thoughts.

David must have been surprised when his father sent for him while he was tendering sheep. Samuel asked the Lord about all his brothers most especially, Eliab. The Lord told Samuel: "Do not look at his appearance or his physical stature, because I have refused him. For the Lord does not see as man sees; for man looks at the outward appearance, but the Lord looks at the heart" (1 Samuel 16:7). God also says in Isaiah 55 verses 8 and 9: "For my thoughts are not your thoughts, nor are your ways My ways, says the Lord. For as the heavens are higher than the earth, so are My ways higher than your ways, And My thoughts than your thoughts".

So, God's jewel, how is your heart? Are your heart and your thoughts pleasing to God? Or are you just marking time on this earth with wicked thoughts and deeds? God does not look at your beauty or appearance or even count on your good works. God does not judge according to your looks or your deeds. He looks at your heart. The Lord takes pleasure in those who fear Him (Psalm 147:11). "Do you look at things (and people) according to the outward appearance?" (2 Corinthians 10:7), Beware, God is watching you and the judgement you are placing on people. God warns you not to judge others because only God sees the heart of the person you are judging. But one thing is also certain there is forgiveness because the Lord says: "For I will forgive their inquiry, and their sin I will remember no more" (Jeremiah 31:34c). He says: "Call to Me. and I will answer you, and show you great and mighty things, which you do not know" (Jeremiah 33:3). God, "give to everyone according to all his (her) ways, whose heart You know (for You alone know the hearts of all the sons of men)" (1 Kings 8:39).

Ecclesiastes 5 verse 2 says that you should not be rash with your mouth, and do not let your heart utter anything hastily before God. The verse says that you should let your words be few. In multitude of words there are sin (Proverbs 10:19). Let God set a guard to your lips (Psalm 141:3). "Keep your tongue from evil and your lips from speaking deceit. Depart from evil and do good, seek peace and pursue it" (Psalm 34:13-14). May God's grace be in our lives.

Be not deceived; God is not mocked you are going to reap what you sow (Galatians 6:7; Colossians 3:25; Psalm 62:12). God is not partial my dear brother and sister. Colossians 3 verse 25 says: "But he who does wrong will be repaid for what he has done, and there is no partiality." and Romans 2 verse 11 echoes this last verse by simply saying: "For there is no partiality with God." Deuteronomy 10 verse 17 supports this point by repeating that, "For the Lord your God is God of gods and Lord of lords, the great God, mighty and awesome, who shows no partiality nor takes a bribe." "Then Peter opened his mouth and said, in truth I perceive that God shows no partiality" (Acts 10:34). Since we have seen from the scriptures that God is not partial, and that we reap what we sow, we should be careful what we are thinking and how we behave. Whatever we sow in our hearts we will reap. So, God's lovely child what are you sowing in secret through your thoughts? Remember, you will reap whatever you sow in secret in front of the whole world. Are you sowing negative thoughts? Think twice because you will reap them with negative actions in the public. "Sow a thought and you reap an action; sow an act and you reap a habit; sow a habit and you reap a character; sow a character and you reap a destiny" (Ralph Waldo Emerson). Be full of Godly grace and character. As Ecclesiastes 5 verse 2 says, "Do not be quick with your mouth, do not be hasty in your heart." Do you have a secret sin you are hiding? Confess it to God now before you are exposed. God is mighty, slow to anger and ready to forgive because of Our Lord Jesus Christ's death and Resurrection. Today is the day of salvation and redemption. Our God is a good, faithful, loving and merciful Father. May the Almighty God cleanse us from all unrighteousness and sinful thoughts Amen. Trust in God do not trust in your own heart but walk wisely under God's counsel (Proverbs 28:26). Let no unwholesome thoughts or actions linger in your mind that will bring shame to our God. Let praise and words of encouragement be in your mouth (Psalm 126:2).

And whatever you do, do all to the glory of God (1 Corinthians 10:31). Do not think in your heart like the king of Tyre (Ezekiel 28:2) and like Satan, that you are God. Do not let your pride bring you to a wrong realization that you are wiser than your Creator: The Almighty God. Lord, constantly sharpen our spiritual appetite so we can continually strive to seek after you and your righteousness Amen. Lord, help us to think Godly thoughts that will reflect in Godly words of hope, comfort, encouragement, love, compassion to others through our voice, through the mail, telephone, emails, words of mouth face to face with family members, friends, acquaintances, co-workers etc. Amen.

Let God perform a spiritual heart surgery in you

As Isaiah discovered in Isaiah 6 verses 5 to 7, God is the only one that can transform and redeem. Isaiah continued to inform us that though our sins be as scarlet they shall become as white as snow, though they be red as crimson they shall be as wool (Isaiah 1:18). This was why He sent Jesus to earth to die for our sins. You are in excellent hands. But one thing is certain. You have to allow God to come into your heart in the first place before transformation can take place in your heart. Do not wait. Embrace God now. Pant, thirst and hunger for God (Psalm 42:1). Have a starving need in your heart for God.

One of the greatest challenges we face as Christians is that of experiencing purity of heart. One of Charles Wesley's Hymns express our heart's desires thus: "O for a heart to praise my God, a heart from sin set free; A heart in every thought renewed and full of love divine. Perfect and right and pure and good; a copy Lord of Thine."

Lord, make my heart a copy of Your Son's. Cleanse us and make us whole by your power and grace in Jesus' Name we pray. Amen. God values a clean heart and cherish Christians with pure motives.

Spiritual health is expressed from the inside out. God transformed the lives of our faith fore-parents. God took Abraham from his unbelieving background and made him a great nation. He can do this for you too. God transformed my heart as a tender young girl and the rest is history. God wants to make us become like Him by giving us 'a new heart' (1 John 3: 2b-3; Ezekiel 36:26). Jesus said in Matthew 5 verse 8 that blessed are the pure in heart for they shall see God. So do not wait. Let Him perform a spiritual heart surgery in you today. God sees us and clothed us in the righteousness of Christ. Because of this, we are always loved and accepted by Him (Romans 4:22-24; 2 Corinthians 5:21).

Focus on living in a right relationship with God. Put Jesus and His righteousness first. Know God. Love God. Hunger and thirst for God (Matthew 5:6) and you will gain and glory in God's righteousness (2 Timothy 2:22; Jeremiah 9:23-24; Matthew 6:25-35). God did it for Peter and He became the Rock upon which the Christian faith was solidified. God did it for Moses and He was a friend of God. He did it for David and he became a man after God's own heart. The same is true about Joseph, Paul, Daniel, Gideon, Shadrach, Meshach and Abednego. Mary's heart was ready and she became the mother of our Lord Jesus Christ. So, try Him. God never fails. Trust your heart to Him and you will not be disappointed. Because God reveals sins like pride, self-pity, complaining, pettiness, prejudice, spite, self-serving indulgence as ugly, ruinous attitudes and actions that we need to deal with. These sins are revealed to us so we can pray and heal. We can pray like David prayed that, "for the sake of your name, Lord, forgive my iniquity though it is great" (Psalm 25:11). David H. Roper of Our Daily Bread Ministries reiterated that, "humbling exposure, though painful, is good for the soul." David H. Roper continued to say that "it's one of the ways in which He God "instructs sinners in His ways and guides the humble in what is right and teaches them His way." Psalm 25 verses 8 to 9 echoes these thoughts too.

As Chris Tomlin sings a song written by Charlie Hall as I wrote earlier: "We bow our hearts. We bend our knees Oh spirit come make us humble. We turn our eyes from evil things. Oh Lord we cast down our idols." Lord transform our hearts and give us clean and pure hearts by doing a spiritual surgery in us in Jesus Name we ask. Amen. Keep your wisdom in our hearts and on our minds O Lord. Amen. And help us to draw on all your resources: Your Word, Prayer, Praise and Gratitude so that we can live a wholistic life well here on earth and reign with you in eternity. Amen.

Do not pretend. Go to God in prayer to confess your emotions to God. Be real and honest about them in front of your Papa. Recognize and understand your emotions and master your emotions with His help (Ephesians 4:26, 17-28; 2 Corinthians 1:21-22). Oswald Chambers reiterated that "it takes the convicting Spirit of God to make men and women know they need to experience a radical work of grace in their hearts." The writer of Every Day With Jesus portrays that, "when it comes to spiritual matters, the heart of the matter is the matter of the heart." So, one thing you should know is that your heart can be transformed. You can have a heart surgery by confessing Jesus Christ as your Lord and Savior and the Holy Spirit can come to reside in your heart and transform your heart and mind. And as Paul says the peace of God will keep your hearts and mind in Christ Jesus (Philippians 4:7). Be real with your Heavenly Father. Pour out your heart to Him, confess your sins and turn away from them, then your hearts will be transformed to be in alignment with what God wants you to be. His child, His friend, His representative. He will give you the desires of your heart when you turn to Him.

Make God the Person to whom you give your ultimate devotion. Do not worship another god as an idol because the thing to which you give your ultimate devotion is the god of your life. That is where you will devote your heart. There can be no real satisfaction in the soul which depends for its pleasure and joy on things and other gods other than God Almighty. Let the touch of God's gladness make your heart sing (Ephesians 1:3; Matthew 5:3; Psalm 128:1-6; Proverbs 15:13; Acts 13:46-52). Rely on the solid Word of God, Meditate and reflect on the Word day and night. Give your love, attention and your whole heart to your Maker and you will be blessed coming in and going out. Keep your eyes and heart on the King of Kings 24/7. Give Him total and not partial control of your heart and it will be well with you. Pour out your heart to Him in humble adoration, praise and thanksgiving. God knows everything including your heart (1 Samuel 16:7). Solomon prayed that God should forgive and act and give to everyone according to all his or her ways, whose heart God knows for God alone knows the heart of all sons and daughters of men (1 Kings 8:39). Trust God with all your heart, soul and being. Give God the key to your heart and He will restore all your lost causes and help with all your problems. Second Corinthians 3 verses 1 to 15 points to the fact that we are Christ's epistles and that Jesus writes His laws into our hearts. Psalm 37 verse 23 points us to the fact that the steps of a good man are ordered by the Lord and He delights in her or his way. So my dear, surrender all to God today.

Be a woman or man after God's heart

David was a man after God's heart (1 Samuel 13:14; Acts 13:22) not because he neither sins nor harbor any sin in his heart, but because he respects the Lord and holds Him as the Lord of Lords and the King of Kings. The Lord ascertain that David will do all His will. God pointed out this fact about David because he was Humble (Acts 13:22). Because he was Trusting (Psalm 27:1); Reverent (Psalm 18:3); Respectful (Psalm 31:9); Loving (Psalm 18:1); Faithful (Psalm 23:6); Obedient (Psalm 119:34); Repentant (Psalm 25:11; Psalm 51 & 32); Devoted (Psalm 4:7) and in addition David recognized the Lord as Supreme (Psalm 9:1). David portrays how we should live as God's beloved. Mary the mother of Our Lord Jesus Christ was a chosen woman after God's heart (Luke 1:26-38) because her heart was receptive to God. As a young girl she loved and held God in high esteem. She also had a love for God's Word as we can see from her reception to the call to be Our Lord's mother and her answer to Angel Gabriel who visited her (Luke 1:38). Hannah was a woman after God's heart when she sang the song of gratitude displaying the knowledge, love and power of God as a holy and just Father (1 Samuel 2:6-7). We too can be a woman and man after God's heart through our humility, obedience, love, respect and reverence for our God and His Word.

Starting today, plan in your heart to become closer to God, read His Word, love the Lord, love Jesus Christ and heed the Holy Spirit's nudges, praise God, show gratitude to the Lord, love your fellow sojourners here and you will be a man or woman after His heart like our fore-parents of faith. Be a man or woman who would do whatever the Lord asks of him or her (Proverbs 3:5-6). Be meek as Jesus said in Matthew 5 verse 5. Meekness portrays the strength of the Lord. Jesus was meek and he showed us the way by becoming human and die for our sins (Philippians 2:6-7). Jesus stripped Himself of all privileges to come in the flesh. Search your heart, my dear sister and brother and ask yourself where do I come short in becoming a man or woman after God's heart? Make amends and go back to your God. He is waiting with open arms to receive you as His beloved. So be godly. The godly are those who are in convenant with God. And they are the recipients of God's lovingkindness.

A merry heart does good like medicine

Jesus repeated so many times that we should "be of good cheer" (Matthew 9:2, 22; 14:27; Acts 23:11; John 16:33). Our Lord Jesus Christ is attuned to what Solomon said in Proverbs 17 verse 22 that, "a merry heart does good like medicine. But a broken spirit dries the bones." Having faith in God gives us a positive outlook on life and keeps us physically, psychologically and emotionally healthy and stable. Therefore, tend your hearts by staying in God's Word and embracing its truths. Your Word have I hidden in my heart that I might not sin against you (Psalm 119:11). With God's Word in your heart and with a positive outlook on the problems that life brings your way, your spiritual lives will become buoyant. The Word will become your source of daily power, encouragement, strength, comfort from the hurts, pains, despair, and frustrations of life. So, meditate on the Word of God daily. Focus on the things of the Lord (Romans 12:2). When your heart is empty, fill it up with the Word of God, Praise and allow the Holy Spirit to fill you up. Be like Christ. Open yourself up to Jesus.

When you accept Jesus Christ as your Savior all things fall into their places within your hearts. You become whole in the Lord. You Grow up wise and do not take life too seriously. Look to God for solutions to your daily problems and like Jesus Christ said: "be of good cheer it is I, do not be afraid" (Matthew 9:2). Look with confidence towards what the day or what life will bring. Cultivate the habit of cheering up on all occasions whatever betides you. This will take a lot of habitual grooming of your life. It will take catching yourself when you do not feel like seeing the bright sides of situations. It will take constant reminding of all the good things the Lord has done in your life and gratitude for all these things. It will take having a heart that remembers all the excellent things God does for you and your family. God has provided us with forgiveness of sin and restored us to Himself through our salvation. This should make us a grateful child of the Almighty that circumstances cannot take from us (Psalm 126:2-3; Habakkuk 3:17-18; Philippians 4:7).

Newton reiterated that: "to take a glimpse within the veil, to know that God is mine, are springs of joy that never fail: Unspeakable Divine!" Marvin Williams of Our Daily Bread Ministries pointed out that: "joy comes from the Lord who lives in us, not from what's happening around us." A heart of gratitude bleeds with gladness and is merry. When you are happy it will show in your face and in your relationship with all those around you. Your attitude to others will be positive and uplifting. You will be like a tree planted by the waters whose leaf is always green (Psalm 1:3; Jeremiah 17:7-8). Richard DeHaan of Our Daily Bread Ministries reiterated that, "Christians, above all others, should benefit from laughter because we have the greatest reason to be joyful." Richard continued further that, "our faith is firmly rooted in God, and our optimism is based on the assurance that our lives are under His wise control." Sper added that, "laughter is a remedy for sorrow and for care; It brings joy to troubled souls, to damaged hearts, repair." So, my dear sister and brother, have a merry heart that will make you whole and to last longer here in your abode as God's child. Research shows that belting out your favorite tune has physiological, emotional, physical, psychological and neurological benefits.

Developing a Childlike, Christlike, Humble Heart

One easy way to simplify your faith is to be like a little child by looking up to Jesus Christ as children look up to their parents when they are young for the supply of their daily needs. Jesus likens greatness to childlikeness. Anyone coming to Him must come in childlike humility, dependency, expectancy, receptivity, faith, and love. We are all referred to as God's little children (1 John 2:1,12,18,28). But we should be careful not to be infants or immature believers in our walk with the Lord (1 Corinthians 3:1-3, 14:20; Ephesians 4:13-14; Hebrews 5:13). We are to be childlike but not childish in our behavior and actions. We should be humble. True humility comes from God.

The example of Nebuchadnezzar in the book of Daniel depicts how pride can lead to failure and a fall (Daniel 3). This king initially acknowledged God as Yahweh: 'the God of gods and the Lord of kings' (Daniel 2:47). But pride in himself and his endowed blessings from God, made him erect a statue of himself which he asked everyone in his kingdom to be in reverence to in place of God (Daniel 3:1-6). While he was boasting in pride he was struck down with a rare mental disorder, boanthropy where a person believes he is a cow or ox (Daniel 4:31-33). He was restored to his sanity after he humbly confessed that

God reigns supreme and when he glorified God again as the King of Kings and Lords of Lords (Daniel 4:37). The arrogant king was able to learn that with pride comes disgrace and a fall. The problem of pride resides in the heart of man. Pride has a way of distorting how we see ourselves. We view ourselves in the mirror of self-importance which makes us perceive a distorted view of who we are. This view makes us think we are more important and greater than our Creator (Proverbs 16:19). Humility offers a realistic perspective of the condition of our hearts (Proverbs 16:18; Matthew 11:29; 20:26-28). But when a man or a woman accepts the Lord as his or her Savior and cultivate Christlike mind, pride gives way to humility (Proverbs 22:4). Our faith in Jesus helps us to become like a trusting child. Greatness as a child of God is childlikeness.

Let the love of God envelope your heart with His peace

Jesus left His peace with us. He does not give as the world gives. He gives His peace to us after we accept Him as our Lord and Savior. We should not let our heart be troubled and we should not be afraid (John 14:27). God cares for us and He instructs us to cast all our anxiety on Him (1 Peter 5:7) for He cares for us. When we are weary and burdened, let us come quietly to the Lord like a baby looking to his mother for comfort and love and He will give our hearts rest and peace (Isaiah 26:3-4). Jesus encourages us in Matthew 6 verses 25 to 34 that we should seek God's kingdom and His righteousness first, and God will add all the things we need, including His peace, to our lives. He is a loving faithful God that stands by His Word. Jesus is telling all the waves in our lives right now: "Peace be still" (Mark 4:39). What are you waiting for? The God of peace is ready to envelope your hearts with His peace.

If you already know Him and do not yet have this peace in your heart, ask for His peace today. If you do not know Him yet, what are you waiting for? Join me and join us and be enveloped with this peace from the Prince of Peace (Isaiah 9:6; John 14:27; 16:33) today. Congratulations!Now that you have asked, seek (Ezekiel 7:25) and get and embrace peace and start pursuing peace (Psalm 34:14). And the God of peace which came to bring peace to us (Matthew 10:34) will keep your heart peaceful in Christ Jesus (Isaiah 26:3; Philippians 4:7; Colossians 3:15). God who is our peace (Ephesians 2:14), has called us to have peace in our hearts (1 Corinthians 7:15). May God's peace which is part of the fruits of the Spirit (Galatians 5:22), fill your hearts in Jesus' Name. Amen. May God's peace be multiplied within your hearts (2 Peter 1:2) in Jesus' Name Amen. And if possible as it depends on you live at peace with all !To live peaceably with all seems like an impossible task.

We share a great testimony as His child when the impossible becomes possible in our lives because of Jesus Christ: The Prince of Peace. Paul was the one that proclaimed that if possible, so far it depends on you, live peaceably with all (Romans 12:18). Peace is made possible by our choices when we surrender control of all situations in our lives over to Jesus, and allow the Holy Spirit to guide us thereby allowing us to live through the leading of His Word. When faced with conflicts and frustration, lean on the Father and pray. Be still before Him and let the Father of peace prevail in your heart as you seek His face (Hebrews 12:14; Isaiah 9:6; John 14:27).

Have a heart of gratitude to God and your fellow sojourners here

A heart of gratitude helps makes life buoyant physically, psychologically and spiritually. Gratitude is the soil on which spiritual joy thrives. Joanie Yoder of Our Daily Bread Ministries reiterated that, "an attitude of gratitude can make your life a beautitude." Be grateful to God and to all those who makes life meaningful for you. Be grateful at all times even when things and conditions look bleak and when there seems to be no hope and no light at the end of the tunnel. Thank God that you are still alive and enjoying His freely given air and all the good things He supplies. "Oh, that men would give thanks to the Lord for His goodness. And for His wonderful works to the children of men! For He satisfies the longing soul. And fills the hungry soul with goodness" (Psalm 107: 8-9). Let men praise the name of the Lord for His Name is to be exalted and His glory is above the earth and heaven (Psalm 148:13). "Let everything that has breath praise the Lord. Praise the Lord" (Psalm 150:6).

Look around for all He provides and seek His kingdom and wait for all other things to be added to you and your household (Matthew 6:33). Do good, be rich in good works and give and have the willingness to share with others (1 Timothy 6:18). "But do not forget to do good and to share, for with such sacrifices God is well pleased (Hebrews 13:16). Wonderful and miraculous things happen when we show gratitude to God and when we find time to praise Our All-knowing Almighty Father (1 Chronicles 16:29 & 34). Jehoshaphat and the people of Judah utilized gratitude and praise to defeat their enemies through the help of God their Helper (2 Chronicles 20: 21-22). Daniel gratefully acknowledged God in the midst of obstacle and unpredictability when his adversaries reported him to King Darius and God honored and rescued him from the lions' den as a result of his faith and gratitude (Daniel 6: 10b & 1-29). Praise allows you to get God's favor and blessings. Paul and Silas, they prayed, they praised and the Holy Ghost came down. So, when the devil brings you face to face with trials and difficulties, just be grateful and praise His Holy Name and you will see His Hand move like He did for the people of Judah and for all those before and after that.

I will praise you, Oh my Savior. I will praise you, Oh my Jesus. I will praise You, Oh my Savior. I will praise you forevermore. Halleluia!It is when we praise God and show our gratitude to Him with our whole heart, that He shows up with His blessings and protection. Be thankful for everything and don't take God and His daily blessings for granted. Recognize and receive God's blessings with grateful hearts (Psalm 103:1-2). His power will flow into your life when you show how grateful you are for His love and faithfulness. In any given set of circumstances, choose to worship and give thanks not to whine, grumble or complain. He created you and fearfully and wonderfully weave you together in your mother's womb (Psalm 139: 14). This is something to shout and praise Him about. You are here on this earth. This is a reason to be grateful. We should give "thanks always for all things to God the Father in the name of Our Lord Jesus Christ submitting to one another in the fear of God" (Ephesians 5: 20-21). Paul also encourages us in 1 Thessalonians 5 verse 18, to give thanks in everything because this is the will of God in Christ Jesus for us. We should give thanks to God all the time for His wonderful works to us as His children (Psalm 107:8).

We should cultivate a heart of gratitude for what God has done in our lives so far, for what He is doing and for what He will do in the future. Say thanksgiving prayers every day. Paul in his writing to the Colossians 3 verse 17 says that, "And whatever you do in word or deed do all in the name of the Lord Jesus giving thanks to God the Father through Him." David C. McCasland of Our Daily Bread Ministries encouraged you that, "thankfulness depends on what is in your heart, not what is in your hand." Thanks be to God for giving us so much to be thankful for. Thank you, Lord for this opportunity to be here and for this one life you have given us.

Gratefulness depends solely our willingness to accept God's will for our lives. We need to accept that our Father, Almighty God can be trusted because He created us and therefore, He is in control of all that happens in our lives. His presence goes with us all day long. God is faithful and He is excellent. We can put our hope in Him to lift us through the strongest storm. Be dependent on God and His faithfulness and love. Always offer love to God in your heart and give thanks for His blessings and the storms that comes to you in life because your sufferings, challenges and obstacles draw you near to God. And they give you courage and strength to move on in life (Psalm 46:1). So, give thanks to Him because He will never fail you throughout your life's journey. Be grateful for His mercy and grace to sustain you and He will see you through because His love and mercy endure forever (Psalms 107:1 & 118:1) and He is good. Like I tell my friends: God is excellent all the time. He gives the best to His children and you are one of His precious children.

The All-Powerful Lord of Heaven and Earth loves you. This is another reason to shout: Halleluia!"Shout joyfully to the Lord, all the earth. Break forth in song, rejoice, and sing praise" (Psalm 98:4). The writer of Psalm 98 praised God for His salvation, His righteousness, His mercy and His faithfulness (verses 2-3). We have a lot to be thankful for. God is a faithful Father who takes excellent care of us His children. Always be grateful. As I said earlier, a heart of gratitude leads to healthy life and spiritual vibrancy, growth and health. Anne Cetas of Our Daily Bread Ministries indicated that, "Gratitude should not be an occasional incident but a continuous (second by second) attitude." Acknowledge God's grace and goodness every second of your days here on earth.

Downplay your self-interest when you give. Give God an acceptable offering from the bottom of your heart. Thanksgiving is a virtue that buds through practice. In a quest to show God your gratitude, list all the basic things of life, the supports you receive from Him and others and the fact that you are alive and breathing and the ability to receive His blessings in your journal daily. Be grateful even for the opportunity to read His Word and this book. Let us bless the Lord at all times and let His praise continually be in our mouths (Psalm 34:1). We serve a living, faithful and joyous Lord.

Let the world know through your joyful exuberance that we serve a living God and that you belong to Jesus. Daniel prayed prayers of gratitude in the midst of despair, fear and unpredictable situation (Daniel 6:10b) and God hears. Abel was grateful for God's provision and God smiled at his offering. Let us cultivate a heart of gratitude for what God has done in our lives, for what He is still doing and for all He promises to do in our lives in the future. Have a daily habit and attitude of gratitude prayers. Yes, You God are worthy of all praise, blessing, honor and glory in Jesus' Name Amen (Jeremiah 31:3-4; Genesis 29:30). Let us not forget that God provides us with all excellent things. As the years add up God's faithfulness and love multiplies. Praise God for all victories, seen and unseen.

Haddon W. Robinson of Our Daily Bread Ministries encouraged us that, if we want to be rich, we should count all the things we have that money cannot buy. Whatever our age, let us make it a habit of thanking God for His greatness, help, provision and companionship. We should continue to praise God because He is in control of everything in our lives and we have nothing to fear. Worship God because of who He is and what He deserves (Psalm 29:2). Give to God and to all those that have helped you make it so far. Give to advance God's cause and to those of the household of God as a way of showing your gratitude.

Love God ! Love Jesus !! Love the Holy Spirit !!!

God is love !

GOD ACCEPTS US AS we are with no pressure to prove ourselves to Him or maintain a status. He loves us in spite of our vulnerabilities, absurdities and obsessions. God is there for us 24/7. "The Lord has appeared of old to (us) saying, Yes, I have loved you with an everlasting love" (Jeremiah 31:3). The fragile parts of our being which God knows, made and understands (Psalm 139:14), is safe with Him. God loves us for who we are because He has a foreknowledge of us (Jeremiah 1:5). He will comfort us, console us, and will be there for us when we are down, and He non-judgementally gives us His unconditional love with no strings attached. God loves you solely because you are you! You are made and cherished by the Almighty God. The more we recognize His love, the greater our trust in Him will grow. What can bring hope for a secure life and be more awesome and comforting more than the reality that God esteems us and give us confidence to be ourselves and live life fully without reservations and restrictions.

God, through His unconditional love, helps us to develop beyond our personal inadequacies into adequate and complete human beings in Him. We are able to have a better life in Jesus Christ because God sent Him to die for us and redeem us from our sins (John

3:16). A God who would give His only Son to die for us simply has to be all goodness. A songwriter put it like this: "God is love, I see it in the earth around me. God is love I feel it in the sky above me. God is love, all nature doth agree. But the greatest proof of His love to me is Calvary." God's goodness shines for all of us to see at Calvary. God is good no matter the appearances to the contrary. The 'old rugged cross' makes that crystal clear. Our debts were settled once and for all at Calvary. We are restored and redeemed. The light came out of the darkness of sin (The old rugged cross, Every Day With Jesus, January 31, 2018). God was the source of this action and move because He sent His Son out of love to die for our sins. As children of God, we have been bought with the precious blood of the Lamb at Calvary. We should be grateful that God is love. Love is the key that unlocks our relationship to God the Father, God the Son and God the Holy Spirit in a relational way. "I have loved you, says the Lord" (Malachi 1:2). "And we have known and believed the love that God has for us. God is love, and He who abides in love abides in God, and God in him (or her)" (1 John 4:16). We should know and appreciate God through the love He has for us. Love is the fulfillment of the law (Romans 13 :10). "Love: which never fails, holds faith, hope and love together. With love as our watchword, we can pray for faith to walk the extra mile and hope that sees the opportunity for Kingdom benefit. Let faith, hope and love provide the trigonometry points by which we navigate our life everyday with Jesus. Build your Christian practice upon the foundation of faith, hope and love" (Colossians 3:14) (Every Day With Jesus, January 2021).

Get genuine and authentic love from your maker the Creator of the Universe

Unless we have a strong conviction that God is entirely trustworthy, perfect and good in character, we will not desire a deep and ongoing relationship with Him. Doubt about God's goodness will lead us to dislike and doubt God and this ultimately leads to disobedience. Eve and Adam did not trust God, and this led to our first parents' disobedience of God. The sinful man is hostile to God (Romans 8:7; James 4:4; 1 Corinthians 2:14; Genesis 3:1-19). Closeness comes when we trust and have confidence in God's goodness, compassion and love. Distance comes when there is lack of trust. Once we love God with our whole heart, mind and soul (Deuteronomy 6:5), God bestows His genuine and authentic love towards us. He cherishes us because we trust and rely on Him solely as our maker and Creator.

Our belief in His goodness and love spurs us on to be closer to Him and to trust Him that He will bestow the best on us whatever the circumstance. Like Job we can comfortably say," though He slay me, yet will I hope in Him" (Job 13:15) and also trust Him. Real love challenges us to fulfill God's plan (Ephesians 5:18-19; 1 Corinthians 12:28; Proverbs 27:17). When we are close to God and have a deep intimate relationship with Him, we may feel downcast but not destroyed.

Distance between God and us can lead to: bitterness, resentment against another person, persistent sin, not spending regular time in God's presence in the Word and in prayers and with other believers. The best way to get genuine and authentic love with Our Papa is through immersing yourself in the Word, through prayers, worshipping God, through fellowshipping with other believers and listening to the direction of the Holy Spirit.

Jesus loves me yes I know!for the Bible tells me so !!

Jesus loves me, this I know

For the Bible tells me so

Little ones to Him belong

They are weak, but He is strong

Yes, Jesus loves me

Yes, Jesus loves me

Yes, Jesus loves me

The Bible tells me so

Jesus loves me, He who died

Heaven's gate to open wide

He will wash away my sin

Let His little child come in

Yes, Jesus loves me

Yes, Jesus loves me

Yes, Jesus loves me

The Bible tells me so

Yes, Jesus loves me

Yes, Jesus loves me

Yes, Jesus loves me

The Bible tells me so

The Bible tells me so

------- Anna Bartlett Warner

Jesus is our all in all, He is everything to us. He is the answer to all our prayers. He is our hope and aspirations. Jesus instructed us to love one another as He has loved us (John 15:12-13). He went on further that by this all men will know we are His disciples if we have love for one another (John 13:34-35). Jesus passionately loves us. This is evident in His decision to lay down His life for us. Our Savior Jesus Christ exemplified His sacrificial love for us by dying for us sinners on the cross. He informed us that as the Father loved Him, so has He also loved us, and He advised us to abide in His love (John 15:9). And since we have been crucified with Christ His love should manifest in us and through us to all around us (Galatians 2:20).

Allow the Holy Spirit to love you and direct your paths

Jesus promised his disciples and that includes us His followers that the Holy Spirit will be our director, teacher, helper, counselor and comforter (John 14:26). We only become victorious when we allow the Holy Spirit to love us and direct our paths in our daily encounters with the world. Holy Spirit come to indwell in our hearts the moment we accept the Lord Jesus as our Savior. To live a victorious Christian life, we need to be sensitive to His nudgings from day to day.

Oswald Chambers reiterated that, "the Holy Ghost is seeking to awaken man out of lethargy; He is pleading, yearning, blessing, pouring benedictions on men, convicting and drawing them nearer, for one purpose only, that they may receive Him so that He may make them holy men and women exhibiting the life of Jesus Christ." Oswald explained further that, "the Holy Spirit is the one who makes everything that Jesus did for you (become) real in your life." Be closer to Jesus and approach God with confidence and ask God for what you need through the Holy Spirit's assistance. Speak fearlessly because you are relating and speaking to your Abba Father, your competent and reliable Father.

God grows us through the difficult times we go through. We and God commune through the help of the Holy Spirit. The Holy

Spirit directs us when we are in oneness with God. Jeremiah 6 verse 16 encourages us that when we stand at a crossroad, we should pray with the help of the Scriptures, stand, look, ask and then walk in the leadings of the Holy Spirit so we can find rest for our souls as we make the right God-inspired decisions. As we read the Word, pray, converse with Godly mentors and yield to the leadings of the Holy Spirit, our decisions become Godly decisions. Proverbs 16 verse 9 says that, "a man's heart devises his (or her) way but the Lord directs his (or her) paths." And as we grow in the Lord, we should pray for our prayer language with which we can communicate directly with the Holy Spirit. This language will help us as we advance in our Christian lives, love others unconditionally and sacrificially.

Don't Look for Love in the wrong places

What is love?

LOVE IS PROBABLY ONE of the most misrepresented words in English language. Love is a mix of emotions, behaviors, and beliefs associated with strong feelings of affection, protectiveness, warmth, and respect for another person. Love demands certain roots to sustain itself over a long period of time. It is always accompanied by actions which depicts the quality of the love that radiates from within. "Love is not a trip. It is not a temporary altered state of consciousness. Love is the brick and mortar of our life, a permanent state and one which we maintain with care. In fact, love never fails. And I can only love others to the degree that I love myself" (Every Day With Jesus, January 2021).

Love is one of the foundational tenets of the Christian faith. Jesus admonished us to love one another and love others as He has loved us. Love entails sacrifice. When we consistently live as God's child in love with Jesus Christ as our Savior, our lives depict and execute actions that depicts God's love revealed through His gift of Jesus (John 3:16). Since God is love, Love is complex and entails a lot of work. We need to understand God's deep love for us in order to know love deeply. And love deeply as God loves us (1 Peter 4:8). Love is an unselfish, affectionate, and benevolent concern for another person and the source of that desire is from God. Jesus loves us unconditionally and gave His life for us so we may attain eternal life. We should therefore be ready to love others as Jesus loves us. Love covers a multitude of sins (1 Corinthians 13:6-8).

For example, a person might say he or she loves God, or love his or her dog, loves freedom or loves different things or persons at different times in their lives. Genuine love is an affectionate and benevolent concern for another person and the source of that desire is from God which is contrasted to the world's idea of love. Love does not come with conditions, stipulations, addenda, or codes and like the sun, love radiates independently of our fears and desires. This as we pointed out earlier, is reflected in First Corinthians 13 verses 6 to 8.

Love is a key attribute of God in Christianity. First John 4 verses 7 to 8 says, "beloved, let us love one another, for love is of God, and everyone who loves is born of God and knows God. He who does not love does not know God, for God is love"; and verse 16 says "he who abides in love abides in God, and God abides in him." John 3 verse 16 states: "For God so loved the world that He gave His only begotten Son (to us) and whoever believes in Him will not perish but have everlasting life." In the New Testament, God's love for humanity or the world is expressed in Greek as agape (ἀγάπη). First Corinthians 13 sums up what love should be within the Christian family. Verses 4 to 5 of First Corinthians 13 says love is patient. Love is kind. It does not envy. It is not boastful or proud. It does not dishonor others and it's neither self-seeking nor easily angered and keeps no record of wrongs. God's justifying love allows us to stand accepted before Him. God was able to make a woman out of a man's rib (Genesis 2:21-22), so both the man and woman can live together in harmony with love for one another.

As children of God, we don't need to search too hard for love. Don't look for love to convince yourself about hidden things like abandonment, loneliness and self-hatred that results from broken relationship, abuse, use of substances or past hurts. Loneliness gives us the most eloquent insights into why love should matter so much. Those looking for love because of loneliness need go no further than to God who has depths of concern, care, attention and love for us. He alone can satisfy our longing and loneliness with no strings attached and without adverse negative consequences as it happens in the use of drugs, or abuse, or looking at the wrong images. The best and only place to find love is from our Heavenly Father who Himself is love personified as we will discuss in the next chapter. God's grace, kindness, and friendship will help you deal with loneliness. God the Father, God the Son and God the Holy Spirit are One. There is unconditional love between the Trinity. And they concurred and agreed and said: "let us make man in our own image" (Genesis 1:26-28). Lord, teach me to love so that others might see the love of God enthused through me and through this gesture, perceive that You are alive. Amen.

We were made to serve and love God

We were all made to serve the Living God. And there is always a hole in our hearts that needs to be filled with following God deeply and wholeheartedly. The Psalmist wrote, "as the deer pants for the water brooks, so pants my soul for You, O God, my soul thirsts for God, for the living God. When shall I come and appear before God?" (Psalm 42:1-2). We were made to thirst for God as the deer pants for water in a brook. Suppressing the thirst for God before we were saved is very common. The Shorter Westminster Catechism asks the question: "what is the chief end of man?" And answers it this way: "The chief end of man is to glorify God and enjoy Him forever." It is when we worship God wholeheartedly that we can serve Him joyously. Life that serves and respects and worship God has the vibrancy that embrace the joy of the Lord devoid of the challenges, struggles and inadvertent mistakes, inconsistencies, lack of faith and lack of the fruits of the Spirit which lead people to despair, hopelessness and emptiness.

Some of us also attempt to satisfy our thirst through other ways than God. We attempt to satisfy the ache in our souls through multiple other ways. In following Jesus more closely, we find ourselves getting more and more in touch with the desire for God that is placed within us. We are implored to reading the Word of God, talking to Him in prayers, praising Him, depending on the Holy Spirit and fellowshipping with other ardent believers. These things become stronger than almost anything we have ever experienced before we were saved (Every Day with Jesus, February 12, 2018). Dear Lord, allow me to have a thirst for you daily in my walk with You. Amen. Only those whose roots reach down deep into God can stand up under the pressures of life.

Let your thoughts be rooted in God's thoughts and your will rooted in God's will. Cultivate your soul to be aligned with what is God's will. Put God first in everything. Be totally committed to God. As Christians, put down spiritual roots. Do not rely on others to be the source of your spiritual nourishment. Draw on the resources God has created and provided for you as His child. Have a close relationship and a daily dependence on God who can be trusted. Draw from the deep-rooted grace and fruitful springs found in God not from the surface waters. Go deep into the knowledge and love of God. Be deeply rooted in God Almighty, the Creator of the world. Love Him with your whole heart and being (Deuteronomy 6:5) and your life will never be the same.

When our spiritual roots go down deep, life's circumstances will not have such a great effect upon us. Rather, we will depend upon God for our support, joy, sustenance, productivity and fulfillment. Our root will be in God not in men or worldly or superficial things (Jeremiah 17:5-8). You will be fruitful. Our true spiritual life should be hidden with Christ in God (Colossians 3:3). Our Spring of Water (Jesus Christ) on whom we can depend solely, will flow constantly. Our streams will make glad the city of God (Psalm 46:4).

Psalm 139 verses 23 to 24; Lamentations 3 verse 40 and First Corinthians 11 verse 28 implores us to examine our ways and pursue a healthy self-examination today. The privilege of bringing our deepest pains, hurts, fears or struggles to a God who cares deeply for our well-being invokes a remarkable feeling within us. The loving compassion of our God is encouraging and makes being a follower of God as a Christian unique. It makes God a perfect confidant to whom we can pour out our hearts and take our heartaches. The book of Lamentations, a book written by Jeremiah to pour out the lament about Jerusalem the 'city of peace,' invokes in us to imperatively check ourselves often and feel the love of God as we turn from our sinful ways. One of the great paradoxes of the Christian life is "to be satisfied with an unsatisfied satisfaction" (Every Day With Jesus, February 7, 2018). Drink constantly from the Living Water. Our Lord Jesus Christ says all those who are thirsty should come and drink from the Living Water (John 4:13). St. Bernard of Clairvaux reiterated that, "we taste Thee,

O thou living Bread. And long to feast upon Thee still. We drink of Thee, the Fountain head, and thirst our souls from Thee to fill."

Do not love the things of the world and its enticements

For those who do not experience the love of God, the grass is always greener on the other side of their fence. Somebody's car is better and shinier. Another friend's wife is smarter. Their children look better. Their houses are neater etc. These are the experiences of someone who loves the world and its enticements. They live by comparisons. The Word of God says, love not the world or the things that are in the world (1 John 2:15). It goes further to say that if you love the world the love of the Father is not in you (1 John 2:15). The love of the world has made so many people lose Heaven and entice the things of the world. It has made them lose Godly wives or husbands and valuable children and family. Beware and be content like Paul entreated us in Philippians 4 verses 11-13.

Most of the time we attempt to satisfy our thirst for God through worldly enticements. Be careful and notice hazards and avoid personal pitfalls like drunkenness and wild living (Ephesians 5:18). Instead seek further to peruse, learn and pursue God's will for your lives (Ephesians 5:17). It is our commitment to independence that prevents us from feeling the desire God puts in us to love and cherish Him. When we can learn to give up our independence and cultivate the habit of loving and putting our trust in God, our soul will come to a place of peace and total dependence on God.

When we accept Jesus as our Lord and Savior, we insatiably possess the desire for things of God. This desire to do things of God becomes stronger than the enticements for worldly things and its enticements (Psalm 105:4; 119:20,13). A follower of Jesus Christ cannot sit on the fence between respecting His values and the values of the world. Francis Schaeffer reiterated that, if the world does not have a problem with us, then, take stock, that might be a warning that we may not be conforming to Christ. When we live in conformity with the Word of God and Christ-laid down principles, the world will not like us because we will not be of the world (John 17:16) and the love of the Father will be in us.

We have to take a stand for God and His principles. And put Him first in everything. Grow in dependence on Christ's boundless power, mercy and grace. Lord, make me a God-dependent person that looks to you and not to the world for my satisfaction in Jesus' Name. Amen (Jeremiah 2:13; Psalm 46:4; John 4:10). Pursue God not the world and its enticements. Pursue God first and totally and all other things will be added to you (Matthew 6:33; Psalm 84:1-2; 143:6). "To have found God and still pursue Him", reiterated St. Bernard of Clairvaux, "is the soul's paradox of love." You can find God and build on your reliance on Him through Praise, Prayer, Gratitude to God for His abundant blessings, immersing yourself in the Word, and associating with genuine born-again Christians. We cannot have, at the same time, equally, the saving friendship of Christ and the hearty friendship of the world. Even when we are shunned and misunderstood or mis-represented we should stand our ground as a Christ-follower. We should stand out and not be lethargic. We should be holy as Our Father in Heaven is holy. We should not have one leg in Christ-kingdom and one leg out in the world. Be wise and be for God and the principles and ways of Jesus Christ who came to save, sanctify and redeem us. We should not compromise our beliefs and principles. But we should also act in love and be discreet towards those who are outside the faith in the world (Colossians 4:5; James 5:7-12; 1 Peter 2:9-17). Be different in a non-judgemental way. Do not cultivate a holier-than-thou attitude. Dear Lord, teach me to live as I should reflecting your power and Your love in the world Amen.

Shun the things of the world and worldliness that are inauthentic and fake love venues

When Moses stayed on Mount Sinai for forty days and forty nights, His face glowed because of God's glory. He has been with God (Exodus 34:29-32). As we spend time with God each day in the Word and in prayers interceding for ourselves and our family members and others, we reflect God's image and shun things of the world and worldliness. We reflect God's love, His beauty, power and grandeur. God can draw others to Himself through our conformity and love of Him and His laws and principles. We will be drawn closely to Him and not to things of the world that are inauthentic and fake love avenues. His Name, love and power stems from us to all those around us and we grow in His grace. You will turn out to be the display of God's goodness and power and radiate His love to others. You will utilize your talents, gifts and abilities to assist others and you will thereby shun things of the world. You will be a conduit of blessings to others who need your experience and expertise to come close to God. You will be a vessel for God and His love will ooze out of you to others. God will work wonders with your life. God will turn all the mistakes of your life into miracles. And make the chaos, mess, confusion, discouragement, sadness, disasters and regrets of your life to become order, peace, love and success when you shun things of the world.

So, shun the unlovable things of the world and go in the strength and power that Jesus bestowed on you (John 20:21). Get rid of all deceit, hypocrisy, envy, and slander of every kind (1 Peter 2:1). And don't make friends with fools so you don't become a fool. "Fools are empty-headed, thick-headed and hard-headed persons who get a failing grade when it comes to the school of wisdom. They may be intellectually brilliant, financially successful and socially admired, but they are morally and spiritually bankrupt (Proverbs 10:21; 14:7). So, when you are forming a friendship, here are some questions to which you need answers: Does the other person bring out the best or the worst in you? Do they have a positive or a negative attitude? What other kinds of friends do they keep? Are they involved in things that violate your values? Do they exercise restraint and control their temper? Do they draw you closer to God or drive you further from Him?" (Don't 'suffer fools gladly,' United Christian Broadcasters/ Word For Today, September 6, 2020). Remember, fools hang out with fools. So, hang out with wise friends and you will be wise. When looking for love, look for wise friends who will draw you closer to God. Because as the saying goes: You are like the friends you hang out with. Shun bad company. Do not be wise in your own eyes. Look for God's best from your friends. The Word says love not the world, for whoever loves the world the love of the Father is not in her or him (1 John 2:15-29).

The love of the world and worldly things portray enmity of God (James 4:4). Put your whole weight on God and His directions as you navigate your journey here and look forward to eternity. Rely on God and His principles as laid down in the Word and not on yourself. Clinging to and relying on things of the world like material things such as cars, houses and women or men will always lead to heart-brokenness. Relying and putting our trust in God first and allowing

Him to add all the things we need for satisfying our this one-given life will lead to peace and lasting happiness. The Word says: Seek first God's kingdom and all these things you need to live a comfortable life will be added to you (Matthew 6:33).

Be led by the Holy Spirit (Romans 8:14). For as many as are led by the Spirit are children of God. Shun self-centeredness and self-love. Let God take center stage in your life. Joanie Yoder of Our Daily Bread Ministries reiterated that "to be under Christ's control is to have true freedom." "Therefore, having these promises, beloved, let us cleanse ourselves from all filthiness of the flesh and spirit, perfecting holiness in the fear of God" (2 Corinthians 7:1).

Love yourself because God genuinely loves you and makes you in His image

Love who God made you to be. You are precious and you are wonderfully and intrincably made (Psalm 139:14). God made you as a special person, one of a kind and He loves all what He made (Genesis 1:31). You should remember this even when you are facing a battle or having a not-so-good a day. When you feel unlovable, God is stretching out His Hand and saying I love you. Even when nobody cares. When your mother or father forsake you (Psalm 27:10) and when the world is turning topsy turvy God is there for you. His love never fails, and nothing can separate you from His love (Romans 8:31-39). This was why He sent His son to die for your sins. For God so love you that He sent his beloved son to shed His blood for you at Calvary (John 3:16). This fact should keep you singing and dancing and holding on to the fact that you are God's jewel (Malachi 3: 16-17; Zechariah 9:16). Praise the Lord every minute of the day because He fearfully and wonderfully made you and knew you when you were in your Mamas womb (Jeremiah 1:5). To help you in your quest and knowledge of how precious you are, ask yourself: How and what do you love about yourself? Take some notes and do not forget to write positive things down because those are the things God remembers and knows and keeps notes of about you. Jot down positive God-inclined qualities. Your uniqueness as one of a kind is noted and celebrated by God. This is what you should celebrate and note too. Forget the negatives that are accentuated by your critics and those who put you down. Emphasize your kindness, your love of justice, love of others and your willingness to help and assist others in need, to mention a few of those characteristics and endowments that our Papa bestows on you. Celebrate who God made you to be: A unique masterpiece. God remembers the kindness you have shown Him (Jeremiah 2:2). So, continue to show God kindness daily.

Find love in the Word, in praying, in praise and in fellowship with genuine children of God

Thine Word have I hidden in my heart that I might not sin against you (Psalm 119:11). The Word of God is the dynamite that destroys all worldliness and negative thoughts in our lives. The Word helps us to advance in our Christian walk. When we read and meditate on the Word we grow and become well rooted in the Lord and the ways of His principles. An important characteristic of a Christian is that she or he receives God's Word and act on it. Jesus said, "for I have given to them (that is, His Disciples) the words which You have given Me; and they have received them, and have known surely that I came from You and they have believed that You sent me" (John 17:8). These words also apply to us as God's children and Jesus's new disciples here on earth.

When we believe and receive the Word of God we will be blessed. Peter, one of the disciples, said in John 6 verse 68 that Jesus had the words of eternal life. One thing we should know is that "to obey the Word does not mean we will never have times of doubt and struggle, but that we hold on to the Word nevertheless" (Every Day With Jesus) and be directed and assisted by its truth. We should keep the Word, obey it as Jesus keeps us (1 John 2:3 & 1-17) and it will be well with us.

Dave Branon of Our Daily Bread Ministries reiterated that God who is the arranger of our world and our society, revealed His desires for us through the Bible. The Scripture, compiled through the inspiration of the Holy Spirit, portrays information about how to live as God's children by obeying His rules and His standards. "The Bible, which is an authoritative Divine revelation of truth, is filled with dramatic examples of fulfilled prophecy. Isaiah 52:13-53:12 and Psalm 22:1-18 record details about the crucifixion of Christ hundreds of years before this cruel form of execution was ever practiced" (Vernon Grounds, Our Daily Bread Ministries).

The Holy Scriptures make us wise for salvation through faith (2 Timothy 3:15). "The Bible is a library of books that includes sixty-six volumes of widely varying length, written over a period of fifteen-hundred years, by more than forty people with all kinds of cultural and educational backgrounds. The Bible is extraordinarily unique and cohesive because the words of each book were 'given by inspiration' or literally 'breathed out by God' (2 Timothy 3:16). Taken together, the books of the Bible tell the story of God's amazing love for us, culminating at the cross. The Bible is principally the story of God's love for you and me. It's a love letter written to us by God. And as you read and meditate on it your fears and worries will be resolved, your questions will be answered, and you will find strength and guidance for daily living" (Have you read your Bible today? United Christian Broadcasters/Word For Today, March 9, 2021). Reading through the Old and New Testament makes us see proof of God's consistent character and faithful love. It gives us the courage to want to live for Him since He knows our names and recognizes us as His blood-bought children.

Proverbs 1 verse 7 says that the fear (and understanding the Word) is the beginning of knowledge (and wisdom, Godly character, living, prosperity and success). While Proverbs 30 verse 5 portrays that every Word of God is flawless, and that God is a shield to those who take refuge in Him. We can take refuge by daily immersing ourselves in His Word. The truth found in God's Word changes everything. We need this truth as God's child as guidance more than ever in a world beset with lots of discrepancies and differing views. Truth matters more than ever. Turn to Jesus: the Way, the Truth and the Life (John 14:6). Good luck as you start eating the Word today as the bread of life, because God's Word is true, as His heart is pure and kind (Psalm 33:4; Acts 14:17). Thine word have I hidden in my heart that I might not sin against you (Psalm119:11). Live according to every word that comes from the mouth of God (Matthew 4:4). Esteem the words that comes from God's mouth more than your necessary food (Job 23:12).

"All Scripture is given by inspiration of God and is profitable for doctrine, for reproof, for correction, for instruction in righteousness, that the man (and woman) of God may be complete, thoroughly equipped for every good work" (2 Timothy 3:16-17). We are encouraged to follow God's message and carry out His instructions as laid out in the Scriptures. We do this through obedience. May God open our eyes so we can see the wonderful and challenging things in His law (Psalm 119:18). The Word reveals the secret about the condition of our hearts (Psalm 25:14; Hebrews 4:12; Luke 1:38; James 1:22; Psalm 119:57-64; Matthew 7:24-27). The Christian life is a race that requires endurance, discipline and correction. The Word acts as our road-map to run this race successfully. You are a success because the Word will show you what He wants you to do, what He wants you to become, how He wants you to behave and all the things He will bestow on you as His beloved child. You will be pointed to God's will for your life as He did with Moses and Joshua and all our fore-parents in the faith.

We need the Word daily to obtain holy striving against self and sin. God-inspired Scripture is a mystery that challenges, chastises, admonishes, encourages and also elicits our Godly inquisitiveness. The Word of God assists us to overcome or better still to triumph over manipulations, dominations and coercions. The Holy Bible is our sword (Hebrews 4:12a; Ephesians 6:11-13). Use your sword because it is of no use until you use it. When we open our Holy Bible we should be confident that it will do what it is set out to do. The Word will cut between our soul and spirit, exposing our innermost thoughts and secrets (Ephesians 4:12). The Word is light to our paths, and it guides our feet (Psalm 119:105). So, hide the Word in your heart to prevent you from committing any sin (Psalm 119:11; Matthew 4:4) and so you can have the peace of God in your heart. The Scripture is for our companionship, information, validation and confirmation. The Word helps us deepen the experience we so much enjoyed and desired. It helps us experience God our Father in a personal and intimate way. The Word allows us to participate in what God has as the purposes for our lives and it offers us His instructions and guidance as we progress in life. When we put what God asks of us in the Bible and listens to what He tells us, we will be prosperous and successful (Joshua 1:8).

Study the Bible. Ruminate on it. Love it as honey on your lips. Make God's Word your daily bread (Psalm 119:100, 97-104, 105-120). Understand it correctly with the assistance and guidance of the Holy Spirit. Obey it and let the Holy Spirit reveal who God is to you and manifest how to follow His instructions through your constant digging into it, since God is truth. His Word is truth and they will be lights to our paths. God cannot lie (Numbers 23:19; Hebrews 6:18). His character is His Word (Numbers 23:19; 1 Samuel 15:29). He magnifies His Word more than His Name (Psalm 138:2).

Focus on God's faithfulness to His promises. His promises to Abraham and all our fore-parents in the faith stood the test of time and came true. You can therefore count on the Word of God to guide you to truthful deliverance in the world because the truth will set you free. God wants the best for all of us. The Bible is a book that will guide us throughout our life. It will never mislead, misinform or misdirect us through its divine guidance. If we follow the truth, all things will work together for good for us (Romans 8:28). The more we carefully peruse the pages of the Bible, the stronger our faith becomes and the more we can worship God in Spirit and in truth (John 4:24). Reading the Bible nurtures our hope in God and make us secure in an unsecure world. It allows us to have confidence in our

Papa who is perpetually in control of the Universe He created and manages with His utmost power.

Immersing ourselves in the Bible and trusting the Father who orchestrates it, allows us to know that nothing can happen to us that God does not know about. Keila Ochoa of Our Daily Bread Ministries encouraged us that "we can dig into the Scriptures and find diamonds of promise, rubies of hope, and emeralds of wisdom." Keila goes on to say that the Scripture points us to the person of Jesus Christ Himself. We are advised to be in the Word every moment we can. Let God's revelation flow into your heart daily from moment to moment so you can know God's will and purposes for your life and thereby make the right choices.

Prayer adds to the growth we establish through the Word. When we pray, we are entreating God to assist us to be fully established in His kingdom as His child and to benefit from all the bounteous blessing He has promised us in His Word. "Prayer is our lesser spirit coming into personal contact with God's Spirit. We come into a common understanding with Him, adjust our will to His will and through the adjustment become more and more like Jesus" (Every Day With Jesus). Alexis Carrel, a Christian writer, says, "Prayer is the most powerful form of energy one can generate." "Prayer produces spiritual strength within us and enables us to rise above the irritations of the day to day and focus on moving from task to task with composure and confidence. The prayerful are sure of their directions, the prayerless are frequently hurried, flurried and worried. Prayer gives us Jesus' awareness and His energy--- and shows us that we have access to the same strength and confidence that filled and guided His life" (Every Day With Jesus). So, cultivate the habit of communing with God, your Creator early as Jesus always did before going into the hurly-burly of the day (Luke 4:42; Psalm 5:1-3; Lamentations 3:22-26) and tell others about the love of God as Jesus instructed (Mark 3:14). Begin by thanking Him for His amazing saving grace and Jesus's work on the cross and for His blessings in your life and your family's life. Organize your day around your prayer not the other way around. Make prayer the top priority of your day.

It is best to spend time in prayer at the start of the day so you can jump-start your day and face the challenges of the day with God Almighty. You go out with God to meet the obstacles or any problem that the day may bring when you approach God at the beginning of the day. Pray for a closer relationship with the Lord and all the things you need will be added unto you (Matthew 6:33). Nothing we do in life is more important than giving time to prayer in an attitude of devotion and thanksgiving (Colossians 4:2). So, cultivate a deeper prayer life to become a successful Christian. We learn to pray for ourselves, our family members and others and receive the results of our prayers. And pray incessantly without ceasing (1 Thessalonians 5:17). This gives us confidence to grow and also become catalysts of change and love for others in God's Kingdom. "Prayer is not a magic wand for satisfying our own wishes, but it's an opportunity to work with the Lord in accomplishing His purposes" (David C. Egner, Our Daily Bread Ministries). When we develop innate relationship with God in prayer, God can drop a word or thought into our hearts that will cause us to be spiritually aroused, reinforced, encouraged, renewed and revitalized in our faith. Prayer turns obstacles into opportunities and disappointments into open doors and appointments. You can know that the last word is with God and not with your circumstances. God therefore dispels the circumstances that are conspiring to crowd or defeat you through prayer and the power that comes from your connection with God. Jesus talked to God all night in Luke chapter 6 verse 12, before He chose His disciples. Prayer makes things possible. Prayer changes things. Oswald Chambers entreated us to pray as God's children. He said we are not beggars or spiritual customers. Oswald went on to say that we should stay in God's presence constantly with our broken treasures or pain and watch Him mend or heal us in such a way and consequently give us the grace to understand God better.

One person has admittedly said that praise steals the avenger. We praise God when we acknowledge His love and faithfulness. Praise allows God to give us more blessings because praise makes God happy and allows Him to perceive the expression of our gratitude to Him for what He has done, what He is currently doing in our lives and what He will do in the future. Fellowshipping with other believers who respect and hold God in high esteem sharpens our faith in God and also helps us as we encourage one another in the faith. Paul entreated us, "let us consider one another in order to stir up love and good works, not forsaking the assembling of ourselves together, as is the manner of some, but exhorting one another, and so much the more as you see the Day approaching" (Hebrews 10:24-25).

So many detours!But one destination !

DETOURS ARE LIKE GOD'S narrow way of opening that point us to the road to the Promised Land. Detour in our lives is like that narrow opening that allows the moth to pass through the cocoon of life to force fluid from its body into the wings so the moth can burst forth as butterfly and fly out for fresh air. If we try to help the moth during its struggle death will result. God allows detours in our lives most of the time to enable us to develop total reliance and trust in Him and make us fly like eagles (Isaiah 40:31). Forcing ourselves out of the detour or not heeding to all the detour signs can prevent us from not fully growing in His love and power. There are times when we stubbornly hit detours on our own. An example of this was when the Israelites spent 40 years in detour for a journey that should have taken them about eleven days. We should be careful that we do not give in to grumbling or complaining or give heed to our stubborn disobedient attitudes and actions during afflictions.

It is imperative to note that Jesus made a risky detour while traveling from Judea to Galilee, He went out of His way to speak to a Samaritan woman (John 4), something unthinkable for a Jew. To make matters worse, she was an adulterous woman avoided even by Samaritans themselves. Yet the detour ended up leading to a conversation that resulted in the salvation of many Samaritans and also opened up the way for the gospel to be preached in that region.

How about Joseph whose story begins in Genesis 37. He had lots of detours too. God had given him two dreams about how his whole family would one day bow down to him. He was going to be a man of power. However, over the next several years, he was sold into slavery by his brothers, and he worked as a servant in Potiphar's household and was falsely accused of attempted rape and thrown into prison. Yes, Joseph's life had taken some seemingly wrong detours, but they were not wrong detours, but "God-ordained detours" to get him to be the leader he was supposed to be. The detours got him to the right place at "God-opportuned-conceived time."

Yes, God uses detours to get us situated in His plan and for His purpose. As the Psalmist reiterated that it is good that I have been afflicted so I can put my trust in you (Psalm 119:71). Be ready to take a risky detour that is God inspired. Who knows, God may be giving you a divine opportunity to talk to someone about Him, today, or meet someone that will lead you to a divine appointment. Put off and discard your old, unrenewed self. Have a fresh mental and spiritual attitude and put on self- generated God-inspired image. Many are the afflictions of the righteous, but the Lord delivers her or him from them all (Psalm 34:19). Jesus encouraged His disciples and us that, in the world we will have tribulations but we should be of good cheer for we have overcome the world (John 16:33). Yes, you have also over-come the world. The Hand that guides you says you have overcome the world.

So, whatever the detours God allows, He will make you an over-comer. He will make you a success and a victor not a victim. The struggle we go through helps us excel as Christians. The detours which can be likened to a weaned child as written by David in Psalm

131 verse 2, assist us to recognize that God is just, loving and considerate (Hebrews 12:3). God's love for us is hard-won, victorious and a love that rescues us. God shows us His character as compassionate, forgiving, just, gracious, faithful and loving as we navigate and come out of our detours. And we can say like Job, He knows the way that I take, and when He has tried me, I shall come forth as gold (Job 23:10).

It is not an easy thing to quieten yourself as a weaned child because we are always impetuous, glamorous, uneasy, in a hurry to mature and also petulant. But the grace of God subdues our soul and make us quiet during the detours of our lives. We are weaned from self-sufficiency, self-will and self-seeking behaviors that result from the things of the world. We learn to bear our divinely imposed cross patiently. We are content with what providence allows in our lives at our abode here (Hebrews 13:5; Philippians 4:11). We learn to depend on God, defer ourselves to God and expect things from God (Psalm 62:5), who then becomes our providence, grace and strength. We defer our will to God and become conformed to His image by emulating our Lord Jesus Christ.

If the Lord makes us go through detours, we should learn to bow to His will without murmuring and have faith that all is well. We learn humility and grow in faith and submit to His will as Jesus did (Mark 14:36; Luke 22:42). We find grace when we learn to lean on God who comforts us when He tries us. Our soul becomes set on things above, on heavenly eternal things and not on things of the world (Galatians 6:14; 2 Corinthians 4:18).

Apple of God's eye (Zechariah 2:8), God rescues you from the fire of hell because of Jesus Christ's sacrifice. He, God, sacrificed His Son for you so you can be redeemed. Remember, there are many detours, but only one destination: The Promised Land, that is Heaven. May God guide us and allow us not to grumble or complain when we hit detours but to look instead to our final destination: Heaven.

Choices!Choices !! Choices !!! Life is full of choices !!

LIFE IS FULL OF choices. Life is all about choices ---- and their consequences. Robert Louis Stevenson quipped that "sooner or later everyone sits down to a banquet of consequences." As children of God, we should pray before we dangle into making choices. Nothing is more important in life than the choices you make. Every poor, wrong or misjudged choice we make gives room to crisis in our lives. Let us look at the choices and consequences that our fore-parents of faith made. With the first couple Adam and Eve in Genesis 3 verse 8, we find out that God does not accept obfuscating, rationalizing, justifying, excusing and blaming as Adam and Eve did in the Garden of Eden (Genesis 3:12). They both got the consequences for their behavior and actions (Genesis 3:15-19). We as humans are still living with these consequences till this day. But praise God we have the choice in accepting Jesus as our Savior to redeem us from these grave consequences that results from the choices made by our first parents. Jacob the trickster got tricked by his sons about Joseph as a consequence of his past tricks on his own brother Esau (Genesis 27:1-28:5; 37:31). On the other hand, Ruth was mentioned in the lineage of our Lord Jesus Christ because she was faithful and loyal to her mother-in-law Naomi (Matthew 1:3-6).

When we choose according to God's will, He will use that choice in ways that exceed our imagination. Choose the fear of the Lord and obtain wisdom to prevent the consequence if you choose not to. When the wisdom of God guides you in your choices you have less reason to fear the consequences those choices might bring into your life. Jesus Christ showed us how to live by doing God's will while He was on earth. He reaped the consequence of following His Father's will by dying for us on the cross so we can be saved from our sins. Lot and Abraham pat ways and Lot made a choice that left all his possessions in flames and even made him lose his wife. Abraham chose the right direction and was content. Beware of greed and coveteousness as you make choices in life. We can also be encouraged by Joseph, Daniel, Shadrach, Meshach and Abednego's choices and the consequences these choices brought them (Genesis 37-50; Daniel 1:8-9; 2:17-30; 6:1-27;).

The writer of United Broadcasters/ Word for Today warns us that we should ask ourselves some cogent questions before we make a choice. "How will this choice affect my character, my sense of self-respect, and my confidence when I approach God in prayer? How will (my choice) affect my influence and respect with other people? How will it affect my family, and those who are following in my footsteps? Hebrews 12 verses 1 to 2 sums up how we should answer these questions in our daily move to make choices when it says, "therefore we also, since we are surrounded by so great a cloud of witnesses, let us lay aside every weight, and the sin which so easily ensnares us, and let us run with endurance the race that is set before us; looking unto Jesus, the author and finisher of our faith, who for the joy that was set before Him, endured the cross, despising the shame, and has sat down at the right hand of the throne of God." You must take responsibility for your life and embrace Jesus Christ if you want to succeed and move forward in life instead of blaming others.

God is ready to forgive you when you confess your sins (Nehemiah 9:17). The bottom line is you must think and pray before you act and consult with and listen to the Holy Spirit before you act. Discern what God wants for your life by praying and listening to His voice through the Holy Spirit promptings and leads. Ask yourself: "what does it mean to hear God's voice and heed His voice and follow where He leads?" Is the choice I am making carnal or Spiritual? Is God embedded in this choice I am making or about to make? Is He with me? If you are hesitant, continue to seek His face, seek Spiritual guidance from the Holy Spirit and your sound Christian based spiritual mentors before you come up with your choice. Let the choices you make be influenced by obedience to God. Look to God and not to your own understanding and in all your ways acknowledge Him and He shall direct your path (Proverbs 3:5-6). Choose to be for God not against Him. If your health allows seek His face in fasting and prayer. Until I go to God, I am incapable of looking at things from God's perspective.

The Holy Bible is full of admonitions and examples of bad choices and excellent ones as we pointed out earlier. Choosing between having something to eat today might mean not having enough tomorrow. The widow of Zaraphath made a choice of sharing her last flour and oil with Elijah (1 Kings 17:7-16). Her choice led to God's divine and miraculous intervention. If she had failed to make this on-the-spot choice she and her son would have starved to death. So, she made the right choice. And the thief at the cross made the on-the-spot choice of believing in Jesus Christ before his death (Luke 23:39-43). On the other hand, Moses' choices prevented him from entering the promised land (Deuteronomy 32:52). David's choice led the prophet Nathan to confront him (2 Samuel 12). Peter wept bitterly after denying that he knew our Lord Jesus Christ (Luke 22:62). As we reiterated in the last section, Moses and the Israelites wondered in the wilderness for 40 years (The book of Numbers & part of Deuteronomy) for a journey that should have taken 11 days, because of grumbling, unbelief and complaining (Deuteronomy 30:19). Joseph stood by God throughout his young, vulnerable life and he subsequently made the right choice that led him to an esteemed position, through patience and endurance (Genesis 41-50). King David's poor decision making had dire consequences, yet God still loved and blessed him with the title, a man after God's own heart (1 Samuel 13:14; Acts 13:22). Despite his poor choices, David was hungry for God, he sought after God, had a passion for spiritual things, tried to please God despite his failures and through his actions he proved he was a God lover and chaser and an ardent worshipper (Psalm 42:1-2). He passionately pursued and ran after God the Holy One whom he adored (Psalm 63:8). Obviously being a man or woman after God's own heart shows us that we do not have to be perfect but to be willing to repent and experience God's plentiful grace and mercy. And even when we make the wrong choices, run to God who is full of grace and mercy.

I am very sure that you, like my humble self, have regretted some choices we made in life. But there is hope. Choose the fear of the Lord (Proverbs 1:28-29) so you can have a Godly consequence (Psalm 25:12). There is a negative consequence if you don't. When the wisdom of God guides us in our choices, we have less reason to fear the consequences those choices might bring into our lives. So what choices are you making today? There are miracles involved in making Godly choices. Choose wisely and do not marginalize yourself from God's purpose. In reality, the choices I make shape my immediate world, influence my behavior which ultimately determines my relationships and the kind of person I become.

Prayerfully consider God and be wise as you navigate the storms and course of life. Let God's Word guide you. It is filled with wisdom and insights for **living fruitful Godly productive Christian life**. His "word is a lamp to guide my feet and a light for my path" (Psalm 119:105). Follow God and His Word and you will never miss the way because where He leads is always right. When you choose God and His Word your way will be clear and your choice will be Godly and God-directed with Godly consequences. Where He leads follow Him. You do not have anything to fear when you are guided by God and His Word. So, choose Him and His Word today.

Oswald Chambers reiterated that, "our spiritual life continually causes us to focus our attention inwardly for the determined purpose of self-examination, because each of us has some qualities we have not yet added to our lives." So, keep asking God for the qualities you need to have, and subsequently for positive spiritual choices you need to make. And with the Holy Spirit's nudgings make the right decisions.

You should know one thing: "there's so much now I cannot see, my eyesight's far too dim; but come what may, I'll simply trust and leave it all to Him" (Overton). Mart DeHaan of Our Daily Bread Ministries entreated us that, "life is filled with unpredictable experiences and events. They (all) seem like stones dropped into the gears of human ingenuity. We learn not to trust our own strength, our own wisdom, or our own skill, but to depend on the Lord who alone knows the end from the beginning." So, when we choose, we should make God and the Word of God the source and ingenious reason for our choice. Mart continued to advise us that "life's race is not over till He says it's over and that living without faith in God is like driving in the fog." Follow God's will. Don't try to make things happen in your strength. Take God's Hand as He leads you and you follow His leads. Obey His instructions as laid down in the Scripture and through Holy Spirit leads. He providentially will lead you to a bright and fruitful, at times through pains and tribulations to a beautiful future. Let His hand be displayed in your life as it was in Mary the mother of Jesus (Luke 1:38; John 3:30; Mark 12:30-31) and Joseph (Genesis 41:38-41) and all our fore-parents' lives. May God lead us to make the right choices that will lead to Godly consequences. Amen. May God give us the grace to yield our lives to His unchanging and faithful care. Amen. May God show us His ways and teach us His paths (Psalm 25:4), so we are not deceived by Satan into making the wrong choices as he persuasively did with Eve and then with Adam (Genesis 3:12). Become God's bosom friend so you can ultimately start making the right choices. Lord, take my life and let it be consecrated to thee (Frances R. Havergal & H. A. Cesar Malan). Be in my choices and lead me aright Lord. May the God of hope make us abound in his love as we make the right choices in life (Romans 15:13) Amen. The wonderful news is that God forgives and accepts those who regret their indiscretions and freely confess them like David did in Psalms 32 and 51. On this same token, although Adam and Eve and we humans faced harsh truth following their poor choice. Yet on the threshold of Paradise God clothes them for the realities that lay beyond the gates (Genesis 3:21). And as I pointed out earlier, God sent Jesus to redeem us of our sins brought on by our first parents.

Bite your tongue!
Hold your peace !!

THE TONGUE, THOUGH ONE of the smallest members of the body (James 3:5) can cause havoc that will make all the other parts of the body cower and run for cover. James informed us that "the tongue is a fire, a world of iniquity. The tongue is so set among our members that it defiles the whole body, and sets on fire the course of nature; and it is set on fire by hell.... But no man can tame the tongue. It is an unruly evil, full of deadly poison" (James 3: 6,8).

The book of Proverbs says those who guard their lips preserve their lives, but those who speak rashly will come to ruin (Proverbs 13:3). The greatest passage on wisdom continued, "Do you see someone who speaks in haste? There is more hope for a fool than for them" (Proverbs 29:20). James admonished us by advising "my dear brothers and sisters, take note of this: everyone should be quick to listen, slow to speak and slow to become angry because human anger does not produce the righteousness that God desires" (James 1:19-20). And "even fools are thought wise if they keep silent, and discerning if they hold their tongue" (Proverbs 17:28). Sharon Jaynes reiterated that "words spoken in anger can be dagger to the heart of the receiver" (Encouragement for Today). The Words of wisdom in the Bible advises us to hold our tongue (James 1:19; Proverbs 15:1,2, 18,31,32,33; 14:29; 16:32). And Paul admonished us in Colossians 4 verse 6 to "let your speech always be gracious, season with salt, so that you may know how you ought to answer everyone." Lord, when criticism strikes, or a dispute hurts, guard our tongues Lord in humble honor of You, and with wisdom let us answer all men and women. Amen (James 1:19-20, 1:5, 5:20; Proverbs 2:6,10:12,18).

Wise living included the careful us of our words. Jesus reiterated that, "a good man out of the good treasure of his heart brings forth good things, and an evil man out of the evil treasure brings forth evil things" (Matthew 12:35). Jesus continued by saying that, "But I say to you that every idle word men (or women) may speak, they will give account of it in the day of judgement. For by your words, you will be justified, and by your words you will be condemned" (Matthew 12:36-37). Before you explode with words in anger, ask yourself this question: What is the reason for my anger? Follow it up with: What will be the outcome of my anger? Will the words I am about to say glorify and edify the Lord and my fellow sojourner? Are the words meant to retaliate against the recipient, make the person feel as bad I feel, shame the recipient, do I want to put the person in her or his place to intimidate him or her? If you answer yes to any of these questions, STOP. Don't move forward with saying anything. Bite your tongue. The Bible said in your anger do not sin (Ephesians 4:26). Paul did not say do not be angry. He said do not let your anger cause you to sin.

Pay close attention to the occasions in Scripture when Jesus got angry (these were few). You will notice that He never became angry over what someone did to Him, He never retaliated or lashed out at those who wronged Him. Jesus got angry over a righteous cause (Mark 3:5; Matthew 21:12). Jesus even prayed as His executioners nailed Him to the cross, that, Father should forgive them for they do not know what they are doing (Luke 23:34). Follow Jesus's examples as His saved sons and daughters. Always wait and pray when you receive or see something that stirs up anger in you. Do not respond immediately. Take a deep breath and let the Holy Spirit guide you in your response. If you are responding to an email or letter read and reread your response to the message or post. Process the response with Godly perspective and pour the water of calmness on the fire of a hot temper. Ask yourself: How will Jesus view this response. If possible, take a walk or move away from the situation to give you a calm spirit. Calm down. Remember: "a soft answer turns away wrath, but a harsh word stirs up anger" (Proverbs 15:1). Use the grace and mercy that has been bestowed on you to respond with grace, truth and love or in some cases do not respond at all. Forever hold your peace and let the peace of God uphold your life and heart (Proverbs 29:11).

Jesus did not answer when He was barraged with cruel words and accusations (Matthew 27:12; 1 Peter 2:23). Don't use words as weapons. Jesus's example and the Holy Spirit's guide offer us a way to respond to people who offend us. The more we are enveloped with His love, the greater we trust and rely on Him for guidance when we are confronted with negative, offending and insulting words from people. Remember, an important but cogent fact: your words shape other people's lives. So, let your words be seasoned with salt so that all who hear or read them become encouraged and uplifted. Let the Psalmist prayer in Psalm 141 verse 3 which prays, "set a guard, O Lord, over my mouth, keep watch over the door of my lips" be daily constantly on your lips. Always remember one thing, "in quietness and confidence shall be your strength" (Isaiah 30:15). So, bite your tongue and hold your peace and you will be counted with the wise as your Papa's child. Do not spend your God-given time in gossips because those who know and are committed to their God-given purpose in life, have no time to gossip (Proverbs 18:8; 20:19; 1 Corinthians 6:19). Use your tongue as a tool of righteousness so you can store up Godly treasures in heaven and allow the words of your mouth and the meditations of your heart to be acceptable to your Almighty Papa, your strength and Redeemer (Psalm 19:14).

Do your work as unto the Lord !

THE MISCONCEPTION SOME OF us Christians have is that we work hard to make money and take care of ourselves and our family. God positioned Adam in garden to tend it (Genesis 2:15). That was his work, and He gave Eve to him as His helpmate in the garden. God sent us here for a purpose and He intends us to be creative, productive, and invested like Him, in tasks that contribute to His purposes (United Christian Broadcasters/Word For Today, December 26, 2020). Paul instructed us to do whatever we do heartily as unto the Lord and not unto men because we will get the reward from Him (Colossians 3:23-24). Do it all for the glory of God (1 Corinthians 10:31). We should take this admonition seriously and do whatever work God gives us to do cheerfully and as unto the Lord serving our bosses and others with God's guidance. God created us to enjoy maximum fulfillment in our work.

Productive work is God's plan for your life. Don't approach your tasks or work with dread or with a desire to escape. Stir yourself up in the Holy Spirit and cheerfully get your work done (2 Timothy 1:6). Work intently and with all your might and power. Serve others well for Jesus' sake and it will count well as part of your eternal reward. A job well done is its own reward too as we journey here on earth. Work gives us a sense of value, without which we can get depressed. We were each created to fulfill a purpose in life, regardless of how much money we have in our bank account. Ecclesiastes 9 verse 10 says that whatever your hand finds to do, do it well now while you are alive. In other words, utilize the opportunity that God gives you now to glorify His Name and to bless those that you come in contact with.

Use your talents to optimize the kingdom of God while you have breath. When you do what you love and love what you do, it becomes your calling from God. When you believe that what you do makes a difference in other peoples' lives, and in your life, you possess a different feeling about your work. When you believe that your job has worth in God's eyes, you will not be vulnerable or sensitive to the critics and/or dependent on cheerleaders. You will look to God as your sustainer and helper. The money you make will make you a contented individual. You will be blessed coming in and going out. So, look to God the author and finisher of your faith not unto men as you perform your jobs daily. Don't work for money. Work to obtain God's glory. So, go ahead, find purpose in your work. Your work is your divine purpose in life.

Face Adversity with Courage !

THE PSALMIST SAYS, MANY are the afflictions of the righteous but the Lord delivers him or her out of them all (Psalm 34:19). James reiterated that we should count it all joy when we fall into various trials and tribulations because the testing of our faith produces patience (James 1:2-4). What we realize is that it is actually when things go wrong that you learn what you are made of and made for. The stuff we are made of and who we believe in are revealed when we face hardships, hurts and suffering. The moment of suffering teaches us and strengthen us. Jesus informed us that in the world we will have tribulations and sufferings but that we should be of good cheer because He has overcome the world (John 16:33). Yes, because we are His, we have overcome the world. Jesus suffered and through suffering He learned trusting and obedience (Hebrews 5:7-9). We need to obey when it hurts and lean on Jesus who learned to obey His Father during suffering when pain and trial rear their heads.

Learn to trust and obey when you face afflictions. Because there is no other way to be happy in Jesus than to trust and obey. Trust. Do not fear (Isaiah 41:10; 2 Corinthians 4:8-10). We bring out Christlike beauty when we are pruned through pain and suffering (John 15:2,8, 1-12). God uses struggles in our lives to produce growth, beauty, fruitfulness, change, strength and to increase our faith (Psalm 80:8; 128:3; Isaiah 5:1-7). Remain steadfast in Jesus Christ during tribulations so you can bear much fruit, share your testimony and become an encouragement to others who may be passing or who will pass through afflictions. The Psalmist says in Psalm 119 verse 71 that, "it was good for me to be afflicted that I might learn your decrees." With all these words of advice, we should face adversity and tribulation with courage and joy.

This is easier said than done because it is difficult to see beyond our nose when we are deep in distress or in suffering. But if we keep the Word of God at the back of our minds, we shall be victorious. Jon Gordon says: "regardless of the adversity you face, your purpose must be greater than your challenges." Jon continued that, "instead of focusing on your problems, focus on your purpose. (And) instead of seeing yourself as a victim, see yourself as a hero. (Because) heroes and victims both get knocked down, but heroes get back up, and armed with faith they create a positive future." Oswald Chambers reiterated that, "we are super-victors with a joy that comes from experiencing the very things which look as if they are going to overwhelm us." Oswald continued that, "huge waves that would frighten an ordinary swimmer produce a tremendous thrill for the surfer who has ridden them." Oswald encouraged us further that, "living a life of faith means never knowing where you are being led. But it does mean loving and knowing the One who is leading." Our teacher in Every Day With Jesus pointed out that "God guides us towards hope and enables us to grasp hope more firmly when he wants to lead us from pain to productivity." This wise teacher reiterated further that, "God permits only what He can use and allow our dreams to be shattered because He knows that His highest purpose for us can best be achieved by so doing" And he concluded that "behind every shattered dream is a reason known to God" which is divine (Plan

A versus Plan B, Every Day with Jesus, December 12, 2017). And even though "sometimes our plan does not unfold the way we thought it would, but God is always in control to use it for our good" (Sper). Because in the drama of life, God is the director behind the scenes (Proverbs 16:9).

As Christians we should be grateful that God knows what He is doing. He has our best interest at heart because He is a kind and compassionate Father whose mercy is new every morning. And no matter what the devil and its cohorts plan and scheme, God is going to see you through all your difficulties and sufferings. Because you believe in Jesus Christ as your Lord and Savior you are overcomers. So, be a conqueror (Romans 8:37). Be extremely joyful in all your sufferings and tribulations (2 Corinthians 7:4). Keep your faith when illness, surgery, financial reversal, or loss of job or any other obstacle threaten you in your life's journey. Dare to be a Daniel, a Moses, a David, a Gideon, a Joseph and a Paul to name a few of the victors and conquerors in the Holy Bible. And you will enjoy God's bounty and blessings. He will restore to you all that the swarming locust has eaten and you will **NEVER** be put to shame (Joel 2:25-27). Bill Crowder of Our Daily Bread Ministries advised us that "focusing on Christ puts everything in perspective" during trials and tribulations. Bill prayed, "Lord, when (our) world is out of control, remind (us) to focus on you --- to rest in your arms and to experience your never-ending grace." Look to the Sovereign Lord for help all the time especially closely in your time of adversity (Psalm 141:8). As Brandt encouraged us, "He knows our burdens and our crosses, those things that hurt, our trials and losses, He cares for every soul that cries, God wipes the tears from every weeping eyes." David C. Egner of Our Daily Bread

Ministries contended that, "during hard times, we face the choice to trust God or to turn from Him." David Egner continued that "if we endure suffering with our trust in the Lord unshaken, we will thwart Satan's efforts and glorify our God."

Stand firm and glorify God as your Rock today and be like the woman or man who build her or his house upon a rock (Matthew 7:24). Lift your eyes higher than your circumstances, higher than your troubles, sufferings, trials, empty promises of the false gods of our day. The bottom line of wisdom is that you should know who you are in God, as God watches our coming and our going today and forever (Psalm 121:8). So, look up today beyond your circumstances. And be comfortable in your own skin and love who God made you to be. His unique and handsome and beautiful child. Take responsibility for your life. In other words, make positive and reliable and realistic decisions regarding your life. Determine what your priorities in life are and will be. Difficulties will come, and when they do show up, **PERSEVERE**. Hang in there by putting your trust in the Almighty who brought you here and crafted you wonderfully and fearfully in your Mama's womb (Psalm 139:14). Let your soul wait silently for God alone because your expectations are from Him (Psalm 62:5). Hardship can prepare us for greater service in God's Kingdom. So, depend on God and refuse to let setback keep you down. Finally, strive to live a life that is truly blessed by God. You are on your way to **living fruitful Godly productive Christian life.**

Confront the Dragons in your life by relying on Jesus Christ: the Champion!

YOU MAY BE ASKING yourself: what dragons. Yes dragons. "Dragons in our lives are the supersized dangers and frailties of life that we're inadequate to fight alone" (Bill Crowder, Our Daily Bread Ministries). Eugene Peterson in *A long obedience in the Same Direction*, wrote that, "dragons are projections of our fears, horrible constructions of all that might hurt us....A peasant confronted by a magnificent dragon is completely out classed."

Life is filled with dragons. These dragons might be a life-threatening health crisis, sudden loss of a job, a failed marriage, strained relationship, or an estranged prodigal child. Whatever the dragon you are facing today, I have excellent news for you. We have a Champion who came before us and has fought these dragons that seek to destroy us or steer us from the course of our faith, on our behalf and made a spectacle of them (Colossians 2:15). Please note that dragons could be of our failures or making or they could be the making of our Spiritual enemy. Jesus Christ who realizes that the dragons might be too big for us came to rescue us and empower us to continue our Christian journey with Him by our side as our Champion. May

God give us the faith, wisdom, grace and power to trust Jesus as our Champion day by day, hour by hour, minute by minute and second by second. Amen. Christ's victory on the cross is enough to crush the dragons that threaten us. Christ in us: the hope of glory. Start walking with Jesus in the power of His might as your Champion today.

Seek wise counsel !

SOLOMON REITERATED THAT THE fear of the Lord is the beginning of wisdom. Wise Christians should therefore seek wisdom. A wise person fears the Lord and does His bidding. They follow in God's footsteps and meditate on the Law of God day and night. Wise people do not follow the tenets of the world. Christians who are wise listen to the advises laid down in the Laws of God which is the Bible and listen to the advice of wise elderly Christians who are strong in the faith. As we mentioned earlier, they pray and listen to the proddings of the Holy Spirit. They will be like David, a man after God's own heart who loves the Lord with his whole heart (1 Samuel 13:14; Acts 13:22). They will refrain from being like Samson who defied his parents' wise counsel (Judges 14:1-19). They will be like a man or woman in Psalm 1 and Jeremiah 17 verse 7 who trusts solely in the Lord and flourishes as a result of their trust in God. They will not relish in worldly things but fix their eyes on eternal glory. They will be blessed going in and coming out. They will seek first God's kingdom and wait for God to add all the things they need to their lives (Matthew 6:33). They will be prudent because as Solomon says in the book of Proverbs: "A prudent man (or woman) foresees danger and take precautions. (But) the simpleton goes blindly on and suffers the consequences" (Proverbs 22:3). Proverbs 13 verse 20 advises us to, "walk with the wise and become wise, for a companion of fools suffers harm."

The wise use their talents wisely and take time for regular disciplined activities and they do something to foster their growth and improve themselves. Author H. Jackson Brown Jr. quipped that, "talent without discipline is like an octopus on roller skates. There's plenty of movements, but you never know if it's going to be forward, backwards, or sideways." Those who are wise improve on their past laurels because they know that improvements require some degree of risk and failure. Keep on improving (Luke 12:48). So, create an environment that will lead to wisdom by seeking wise counsel and delving on the Word of God and listening to the nudgings of the Holy Spirit.

Pray for the patience of Job

ONE OF THE THINGS I am learning at this season of life is how to have patience. Patience is also brewed out of finding reasons to be thankful (1 Thessalonians 5:16-18). This means not complaining, not worrying, not finding excuses, not relinquishing our faith in the Almighty. Noah learned to wait on the Lord when He was told to build the Ark (Genesis 8:10-11). Wait on the Lord, be of good courage, and He shall strengthen your heart. Wait I say on the Lord (Psalm 27:14). Be still and know that God is God (Psalm 46:10). God informed the Israelites to wait in front of the Red Seat and perceive His glory and see His goodness (Exodus 14). Sarah was like all of us. She could not wait. She had to have Hagar bear a son on her behalf. Job on the other hand waited patiently and saw God's Hand move in miraculous ways. Daniel waited quietly in the lions' den without fretting and you read what happened (Daniel 6). God proved Himself to Daniel and the king took notice of this God who saves. When God seems silent, He is up to something good on your behalf. Joseph waited for 14 years before his destiny was fulfilled. Joseph's patience, trust and faith in the Almighty were rewarded with prestigious position unheard of for a Hebrew son. Joseph's patience made him save his brethren and all their family members.

Focus on God. Wait. If you wait on the Lord, God will give you His peace which passes all understanding. Hold on to the Lord and He will give you peace especially in times of adversity and trials.

God will bestow us with His peace and help us in times of trouble. Through this holding on to the Lord our patience will grow. We can learn from the stories of those who waited and still wait on the Lord as well as those who could not patiently wait but want to help the Lord. Those who could not wait go past their blessings or their blessings go past them. Those who waited patiently reaped the fruit of patience.

So, how do you gain patience? Through constant prayer and listening intently to the Holy Spirit and saturating yourself in the Word of God. It is a good idea to memorize some verses of the Holy Bible and bring them to remembrance when you are apt to act in haste or become impatient. Like you, I am learning and praying for patience. May the Almighty help us to have the patience of Job. Amen. The Word of God in Deuteronomy 31:6; Psalm 138:8a; Romans 8:28; John14:27; 1 Peter 5:7; Matthew 11:28-29; Matthew 6:35-34 and Psalm 91:2 will assist you as you patiently seek God's face with patience.

Conclusion

OUR GOD, WHO CREATED the Universe, and who knits you together in your mother's womb is a competent and reliable Father. He loves you and wants you to realize that this love is everlasting and does not change. He wants you to trust Him too. Rely on Him, embrace Him, acknowledge Him and you will have life and this life abundantly (John 10:10).

After reading about our Heavenly Father, you have discovered that no one, yes no one, compares to Our Papa who is in heaven. We should love Him, respect Him and stand in awe of Him. We stand we stand in awe of you. Holy God to whom all praise is due we stand in awe of you. If you do not yet know Him this is your chance. This is your opportunity. Bow your head and allow Him the honor of becoming your Father. Your Father in Heaven loves you and He is waiting with open arms to welcome you into the fold of His beloved children. His love is incomparable to anything you have ever known. Yes, no other love can compare to His love for you.

According to the Word of God the human "heart is deceitful above all things. And desperately wicked; who can know it?" (Jeremiah 17:9). But the Word continues that "I, the Lord search the heart, I test the mind. Even to give every man according to (her) or his ways, according to the fruit of his (or her) doings" (Jeremiah 17:10). But there is hope as we can see from the God's Word and from the discussions in the chapters above. God can do the spiritual surgery if we allow him to, and trust in Him. Because, "blessed is the man (or woman) who trusts in the Lord and whose hope is in the Lord" (Jeremiah 17:7). The Word of God likens that woman or man to a tree planted by watery forest whose plants are fruitful (Psalm 1:1-3; Jeremiah 17:8). So, where does your heart want to be rooted in? In green pastures or in dry land? Cursed or Blessed? Choose life and live abundantly with Jesus Christ (John 10:10). Be a woman and man after God's own heart like David (1 Samuel 13:14; Acts 13:22), and Mary the mother Our Lord Jesus Christ and all our fore-parents of faith. Let the fruits of the Spirit, which is love, joy, peace, longsuffering, kindness, goodness, faithfulness, gentleness and self-control spring forth in your heart (Galatians 5:22-23). I pray that you allow your heart to be spiritually attuned to God's Word and principles so you can enjoy life here with Him and also in eternity in Jesus' Name Amen.

I also pray that God's love will radiate into your heart and that God will envelope you with this love so that you become embolden to tell others about this great love. *Guide to living Fruitful Godly Productive Christian life* has allowed you to see that love is not love until you give it away after getting it from your Heavenly loving Father. This enriching book has also alerted you to important nudgets that will allow you to live fruitful Godly productive Christian life. May God bless you as you make the choice to look for and embrace your Papa's love. Amen. May God give us the grace to trust, love and have faith in Him more day by day. May we have the grace to trust Him more and more because it is so sweet to trust Jesus and the Lord. And this we all know very well that, because he lives, we can face tomorrow. Because he lives all our fears are gone. And because we know He holds our future. Our life is worth living just because he lives.

OTHER BOOKS BY MARY OLUFUNMILAYO ADEKSON (Faith Diversity Consulting)

You only live once: Live for God

Prayer: The Christian's Anchor

God's Masterpiece

God Inspired Devotionals from the Praying Mother (Iya Aadua)

Thriving After Divorce

.

www.ingramcontent.com/pod-product-compliance
Lightning Source LLC
Chambersburg PA
CBHW031954080426
42735CB00007B/391